Oh, the Things They Like to Hide

A doctor's battle to save lives
in the midst of political scandal during
our nation's opioid epidemic

Dr. B. Sky

ISBN 978-1-64515-384-9 (paperback)
ISBN 978-1-64515-385-6 (digital)

Christian Faith Publishing, Inc.
832 Park Avenue
Meadville, PA 16335
www.christianfaithpublishing.com

Printed in the United States of America

To all of the medical providers who battle political influences in their practices and persevere. May the Lord grant you wisdom, courage, and faith in his promises to bring justice to all and glory to God. May we all recognize and cherish the values of integrity, commitment, advocacy, respect, and excellence. I praise God for his mercy, grace, and love.

CONTENTS

ACKNOWLEDGMENT

First, I give glory to God and his faithfulness to bring good out of evil. May the telling of this battle inspire others to look above and into God's Word for encouragement and guidance as we confront the enemy.

To all of my dedicated staff and colleagues, I thank you for your words of encouragement, constant support, and prayers.

To my attorney, I will never forget our first conversation, and you "got it!" Your belief in opioid safety motivated me to continue to advocate for patients and the community with the aspiration of saving lives.

To a special colleague, thank you for the title of this book, for my alias, and for inspiring me to write. God has truly blessed us for our faithfulness and led us to greener pastures.

To my family and dear husband, I praise God for you and for loving me, "just the way I am." You all allow me to be me, and you actually believe I am doing the right thing, even when the seas get rough and the roads gets rocky. In the end, I am merely seeking God's plan for my life, and you all happen to be along for the ride as part of his plan for your lives. Isn't that wonderful?

This is a true story about politicians, a large health-care system, coercion, and how unsolicited political pressure placed upon physicians and providers can thwart efforts to apply opioid safety initiatives in America leading to unintentional drug overdoses.

PREFACE

Wherefore seeing we also are compassed about with so
great a cloud of witnesses, let us lay aside every weight,
and the sin which doth so easily beset us, and let us
run with patience the race that is set before us.

—Hebrews 12:1, KJV

I was praying one day and suddenly felt the need to uncover the influence of politicians and their contribution to the opioid crisis in the United States. I battled opioid safety for our patients for over fifteen years, first as a primary care provider by the Great Lakes, later as the primary and specialty service line director in the middle of a cornfield, and lastly as the associate chief of staff for primary care in a river city. My battle ends in the river city following a very eye-opening experience involving a newscaster, Ignorant Oversight Body, director, chief of staff, and a politician from the river city. This is my story.

INTRODUCTION

I can do all things through Christ which strengtheneth me.

—Philippians 4:13, KJV

First, let's begin with my background. I attended medical school at the age of thirty, a time when everyone thought this was too old to pursue such a lofty career. I defied the allopathic (MD) schools after multiple rejections due to my age and other political influences at that time which pales to my current story, so we will skip that part of my life. The Osteopathic University, in the land of wheat field farmers, welcomed me with open arms during my site interview visit. Two weeks later, I was on my way to the wheat fields in my little Chevy Sprint. I packed my car fully, every square inch of the interior filled with my possessions. My bike hung on the back bumper. Wilamina, my momma lab rat, rescued after I killed her babies in the name of a science research project, slept on the front passenger seat. Yes, another story to tell at another time. I graduated third in my class which began with 171 students. That was a fun day, graduation day, when the top three students were announced. No one expected me, a fairly good-looking blonde at the time I guess, to be smart. I spent my whole life proving that blondes can be smart, defying the stereotype that still exists today. I am a brunette now for such reasons. I grew tired of having to prove my intelligence to sceptics who constantly judged me by my appearance.

Following further training, I served in the military as a general medical officer. I joined during the first Gulf War, and my mom cried. I always yearned to serve my country in the armed forces since childhood. I remembered the *Sonny and Cher Show* when they showed their POW bracelets, and my mom had the same one as Sonny or Cher. I felt for those who fought in the war. Vietnam was such a terrible place to serve, so much tragedy. Brave men and women served only to come home to a country who spat on them. I wanted to take care of them, initially as a counselor or psychiatrist. I was driven to fulfill this dream.

Stationed at a submarine base on the coast, I enjoyed working as a general medical officer in the Acute Care Clinic treating active duty service members, their families, and retirees. Married at the time, I ultimately survived a terrible divorce when my husband and his family insist I "quit" the military, stay home, and have babies. First of all, I could not "quit" the military without spending time in Leavenworth. Their expectations astonished me, and it took removing me from my country to "visit" the Philippines, their "home," and make these demands when I had no support system. I barely made it home. After a total meltdown, I found myself at an overcrowded airport, the only blonde Caucasian female amidst a sea of Filipinos and Filipinas, at the end of an unending line and no ticket. I didn't even know how to make a phone call. I made it "home" to the United States three days later.

When I completed my service obligation, I sought after my dream of solo general medical practice in a small tourist town on the east coast. Mistake number one was being a young blonde female in a town of older established good ol' boys. I did not fit in at all. The hospital wanted me there but nobody else. After one year of being "on call," twenty-four seven on call, 365 days per year, I wanted out. I stayed three more years. I loved my patients, and I did not want to leave them. Eventually, I had to leave them because there was nothing left of me. I gave my everything to everyone else, and I knew I had to find some support elsewhere.

I went home for Christmas in December of 2001. Home at the time and for most of my life was on the Great Lakes. My mom still lives there. I still have most of my friends in that area as does my husband, David. I had not met David yet. He comes into my life a little later, but not much later. I thought to myself at that time, *well,*

I loved being a military doctor, so why don't I check out the large health-care organization? I walked into the organization and asked about opportunities. I was basically hired on the spot. I ran into the right people at the right time in the human resources department. The next day, I interviewed with the chief of staff and others. I think they hired me based upon my board scores. The chief of staff, who is still in this position today, and others alluded to this outstanding achievement, and I knew my life was about to change. Finally, I would be part of a group of physicians with a support system and no "on call" as an outpatient physician for two outpatient clinics (OCs). I felt relieved and rejuvenated.

I started closing my practice by choosing not to bill insurance companies. My business became a cash practice, and I knew patients would choose to go elsewhere. I felt less guilty starting out this way rather than simply closing my doors. In the end, quite a few patients stayed with me. The number of letters and chart copies I had to send out in the end were more than I imagined. My best friend's daughters helped me stuff envelopes and place stamps for mailing the announcement of closing my practice.

A friend of mine was being baptized by the Great Lakes, so I took the opportunity to move some of my belongings, and I attended church for the baptism. I found a wonderful Baptist church during my first visit, so I knew I would have a church family. After a long day and a date with a guy my friends tried to fix me up with, I sat at my mom's house discussing the day and future plans. The phone rang. It was David, the man my mom wanted to fix me up with, but I was resisting at the moment. He sounded nice. He invited me out for coffee. I hesitated because I was leaving for the east coast early the next morning. I agreed to meet him for coffee. Caribou Coffee was closed, so we went to the bar next door and drank coffee, for hours. First of all, David was as handsome as could be, a "cutie patootie" I would soon tease, drove the same color vehicle, and fell for me as quickly as I fell for him. He got me at "I would have taken a bullet for her" (his ex-wife).

I drove back to the east coast. It was hard to go back; but it had to be done. David called me that night and almost every night since. We have been happily married for fifteen years now.

CHAPTER 1

Welcome to the Large Health-care System

The LORD is my rock, and my fortress, and my deliverer;
my God, my strength, in whom I will trust; my buckler,
and the horn of my salvation, and my high tower.

—Psalm 18:2, KJV

I inherited a panel of patients on opioids for chronic pain for years. I rarely prescribed opioids for chronic pain. This practice surprised and disturbed me. A previous physician, known as the "candy lady," prescribed opioids regularly for chronic pain. Patients loved her, and who wouldn't when she would give you whatever you asked for to make you happy? Seriously, as a medical doctor, how could you practice like this woman? I simply never fell into that line of thinking. Many medical doctors did though innocently enough, and really, I can see why this happened, especially at the large health-care system. I really get it now!

In the 1990s and until fairly recently, we, the medical profession, used a pain score as the fifth vital sign. The goal was to get everyone's pain as close to zero as possible. We know now that this is not how pain works. When you bring in the influence of pharmaceutical representatives touting how medications such as tramadol do not have addiction potential and patients ask for more and more, it does not take a rocket scientist to question the potential for addiction to tramadol, now grouped with "opioids" as far as addiction potential goes. I remember this one in particular because it was easy to see the drug-seeking behavior of patients on tramadol and other opioids.

As physicians and providers, we first tried to eliminate fast-acting opioids except for breakthrough pain. We changed our prescriptions to long-acting opioids and decreased the number of immediate-release pills dispensed. When these did not work to get patients' pain to zero, we started using fentanyl patches and then methadone because it was cheap. I say we, but I can honestly say I fought doing any of this my entire career. This type of prescribing was accepted as standard of care at the time overall. However, there were those medical practices that were considered conservative, such as mine, and others who were outliers. These outliers numbered more than I could ever believe in my naivety.

Medical practices started making the news headlines, especially pain medicine practices. Physicians lost their licenses. Some lost their licenses by exchanging sex or other favors for opioid prescriptions; others became addicts themselves; still others sold opioids for profit; and some simply failed to inform their patients of the potential for opioid addiction, even in the face of using them properly in acute situations. These are the providers I feel for most of all. We did not know much about the abuse potential of these medications as caring providers. We were just trying to get pain levels to the impossible goal of zero! We were harshly judged by inspection oversight bodies who reviewed quality measure statistics and rated doctors poorly, publishing results citing failure to eliminate pain in their patients. Providers were pressured, judged, and expected to do the impossible. Physicians, criticized by nonclinical quality of care reviewers, utilization managers, and others, fell into the opioid-prescribing trap. We were "damned if we did" and "damned if we didn't" prescribe pills in an effort to eliminate chronic pain.

My boss inherited the candy lady's panel of patients first. She tried to decrease the doses to some degree, I am certain. She knew why that physician was no longer with us at the large health-care system. I remember my boss signing a stack of opioid prescriptions prior to her scheduled leave. She realized some of us would not want to address this situation, especially me. Eventually, my boss received a promotion at another facility within the large health-care system, and I inherited those patients on opioids. Lucky me.

When I reviewed the charts on my new patients, I noted that many of them had been on these medications for years and years without further evaluations of their pain. I started with evaluations. I joined a team of providers who met by clinical video regularly to review chronic pain patients to establish a treatment plan, and this included addressing opioids. The team consisted of the associate chief of staff (ACOS) for primary care and an anesthesiologist serving as the pain management provider. (These two physicians are still in their same positions.) The team also included a pain psychologist, a substance abuse specialty psychiatrist, pain management nurse who documented the meetings, and the primary care providers of the patients discussed. At other times, the patients could meet with the pain management team by clinical video telehealth at remote locations. Prescribing patterns of providers were monitored, and they were offered continuous education about opioid safety and alternatives in caring for chronic pain patients. Resources went into the development of a specialty pain clinic where patients could be referred. The program worked. To this day, this facility has very few patients on opioids for chronic pain. I feel proud to have started my journey with this group of providers.

I used my GI Bill and earned a MBA in health care from a local college. I studied with leaders sent by prestigious medical centers. Additionally, I was selected to participate in a highly regarded leadership training program for the organization. My desire as a leader was to advocate for what I call "frontline" staff (those employees directly caring for patients) and ensure the participation of frontline clinicians and other clinical staff during administrative discussions and planning. As a frontline staff advocate, I understood I could make a difference in the health-care system, at least in my small area of influence.

CHAPTER 2

Moving on up in the Name of Advocacy

Looking unto Jesus the author and finisher of our faith; who for the joy that was set before him endured the cross, despising the shame, and is set down at the right hand of the throne of God.

—Hebrews 12:1, 2, KJV

My first vast administrative position brought me to the land of cornfields and soybeans. I loved it. Appointed primary and specialty medicine service line director, I accepted responsibility for oversight of the ICU, emergency department, hospitalist program, primary care, and many specialties. I didn't realize the scope of this challenge. Good thing because I would have tucked my tail between my legs and rushed back to the Great Lakes.

I discovered our pain management psychiatrist doled out opioids by the dozens and even hundreds. He fell into one of the unfortunate categories previously mentioned, and soon, all of the prescribing fell onto the chief of staff. I witnessed the stack of opioid prescriptions the chief of staff would sign during meetings, and it reminded me of having to write repetitive sentences on a blackboard as punishment in the old days. I could tell he did not want to do this; but he felt like he had no choice. The chief of staff participated in the regular educational sessions for these patients. Our facility tried to educate the chronic pain patients on opioids by requiring attendance at these educational meetings; but the meetings did not appear to be effective. Eventually, the chief of staff reassigned pain management to the primary and specialty service line. This meant I was now in charge. I boldly stated that I would not be signing prescriptions. I convinced my colleagues that a better way of doing business existed. Fortunately, another psychiatrist took on the pain prescription reviews, and we teamed up with my primary care providers to make changes. Additionally, a group of us service chiefs and others across a multidisciplinary medical group including pharmacists, mental health providers, physiatrists, surgeons, nurses, primary care providers, and others met weekly and later monthly to design a fully functioning pain clinic. It took us two years of meetings, hard work, and strategic planning; but we succeeded. When I left the land of corn and soybeans, I left a fully functioning pain management clinic consisting of pain clinical pharmacy specialists, physiatrists, substance abuse psychologist, chiropractic care, acupuncture specialist, two pain primary care providers, and nursing and clerical staff. Our use of opioids for chronic pain plummeted. Policies, procedures, and processes solidified the plan for success and sustainment.

In the fall of 2015, a facility by the river recruited me to join their team as the associate chief of staff (ACOS) for primary care and, shortly after my arrival, the opioid safety initiative facility prescribing champion. The chief of staff at that time along with the director accepted other opportunities within the large health-care system and departed by the time I arrived or shortly after. The deputy chief of staff acted as the ACOS for primary care prior to my arrival. He soon became the acting chief of staff for the facility and then the chief of staff. I liked him as a person. I was less certain about my thoughts regarding his leadership ability. I felt like I coexisted with the chief of staff, educating and directing him about policies, procedures, and processes of the large health-care system to keep him away from turmoil or at least scrutiny.

Initially, I was delighted to aid the chief of staff; but later, delight turned to distress when the chief of staff threw policy and procedure out the window and acted upon ludicrous orders commanded by an uneducated director. I became a political target.

My previous experiences and educational opportunities at the large health-care system were abundant. I attended many leadership training classes regarding the large health-care system's structure, leadership, mission, values, characteristics, and goals. I participated in union, human resource, credentialing and privileging, compensation and pension, telemedicine, strategic initiative planning, systems redesign, and other leadership training opportunities. Unfortunately, at times, I needed to put what I learned into practice. My presence during a plethora of inspections including but not limited to Joint Commission, regional quality inspections, internal inspectors, Office of Accountability, and other oversight bodies added to my education and large health-care system leadership experience. Sometimes I shined, and other times I suffered, especially when I had to deal with a group of investigators who said, "Now I am asking you for the third time," as if declaring I was deceitful when I stated my previous answer repeatedly. It was like the question, "when did you quit beating your wife?" and you never laid hands on your wife. I fared well with investigations overall, and my executive leadership team in the land of corn and soybeans supported me. The Facility by the River (FBTR) executive leadership team would prove to be different, very different.

CHAPTER 3

The State of the Facility by the River (FBTR)

Being confident of this very thing, that he which hath begun a good work in you will perform it until the day of Jesus Christ.

—Philippians 1:6, KJV

I relocated to the river area to work as the associate chief of staff (ACOS) for primary care. I learned immediately that primary care provider turnover was ridiculously high. The facility lost sixteen providers prior to my arrival within a very short amount of time. The previous ACOS for primary care and the two clinical managers for primary care were all detailed to care for patients on a full-time basis. The deputy chief of staff was detailed to acting ACOS for primary care. This detail becomes a significant factor in my story. The primary care administrative officer for primary care changed positions, and the job was vacant. The only clerical support for primary care was filled at a remote location. This facility consisted of multiple inpatient units, outpatient departments, and outpatient clinics (OCs) traversing the state at multiple locations. The clinical manager for the outpatient clinics (OCs) left her position also. The former ACOS for primary care quit coming to work prior to and during my initial time at this facility. Other primary care providers called in sick regularly which I quickly learned was due to provider burnout. This facility performed well on access measures and other quality data reviews. The senior leaders bragged about their success; but their success cost the facility sixteen primary care providers including four primary care leaders.

Clinical chart reviews, provider proficiencies, and ongoing/ focused professional practice evaluations (OPPEs, FPPEs) for credentialing and privileging had not been completed for at least a year on any of the primary care staff. Provider schedules had four overbooks a day. Clinical alerts requiring action by the clinical staff went unanswered for months. Some of the providers had more than two thousand clinical alerts unanswered, and one provider had over five thousand unanswered clinical alerts, many requiring action to help patients. When providers called in sick, the alerts went to a surrogate. The ACOS for primary care quit coming to work a month or two before I arrived, and his surrogate was totally overwhelmed and relocated to another facility shortly after my arrival. One of my clinical managers tried to help, but she soon suffered a mental crisis and left due to burnout. I subsequently addressed hundreds to thousands of alerts myself in an attempt to get our providers back on track. This also becomes a crucial factor in my story.

I provided clinical assistance for many different facility locations. We were sinking fast, and the patients were suffering. Sure, we could get them in to be seen by allowing four overbooks a day, but the limited number of providers could not follow up on much, and it became easy to miss an important radiology or lab result. Attending to prescription refill requests, patient advocate inquiries, nursing notes, and other action items became difficult, and the number of unattended alerts grew. Other providers could not keep up with their notes and billing encounters, and they were constantly hounded by nonclinical staff. The providers would call in sick just to catch up on alerts for survival. I am sure many other providers wanted to leave this crazy system; but they could not leave due to personal obligations. I stayed to assist and advocate for the primary care providers and other frontline clinical staff. My goal was to make their jobs easier so they could care for the patients. What a challenge!

I worked well into every evening and on weekends assisting patients and providers for at least six months following my arrival. I convinced the chief of staff to allow providers administrative time to address clinical alerts. He agreed to two hours weekly initially, and eventually, I was successful in getting four hours weekly. I insisted on stopping overbooks. I spoke often about provider burnout reviewing the list of lost primary care providers with the chief of staff and acting directors. It thrilled me when the chief of staff began researching and discussing provider burnout at medical staff meetings. This was and still is known to be a real problem at the health-care system nationally. Turnover is real! Turnover affects access! Turnover affects care of our patients!

Soon, I earned the respect and trust of the primary care staff. The proof was evident in the data on the employee survey (ES). We rocked! Our facility was known to be the one of the most improved nationally on the survey in 2016. Primary care scores contributed greatly. Our service line hired new providers. We had a great reputation regarding treatment of our staff in primary care. We were almost completely staffed in March of 2017 and only waiting for a couple of physicians to relocate. We had two administrative officers for primary care at two locations. Our administrative staff worked well together and supported one another. We celebrated our success.

The Drug Enforcement Administration (DEA) investigated our health-care system in the late fall of 2015, just after I arrived. Since I was new, I did not participate in the interview. The chief of staff was acting ACOS for primary care. He provided oversight in some regard for two years prior to my arrival as acting ACOS for primary care and deputy chief of staff. He was in charge of opioid safety initiation, and just as he failed to keep up on proficiencies, medical chart reviews, ongoing professional practice evaluations, and other duties, he failed to initiate opioid safety initiatives to any significant degree. The only safety initiatives performed were pain agreements which were meaningless because when patients complained about agreement violation consequences, the former chief of staff and deputy chief of staff had discussions with the primary care providers to "encourage" reinstatement of the opioids. I heard this over and over again upon my arrival and assured the primary care providers this would no longer occur. I offered to be their support person with any questions stating that nobody can "make" providers prescribe a medication against their better judgment, even me. This type of action is illegal.

The internal inspectors arrived to evaluate the facility's dispensing pattern and use of opioid medication in the spring of 2016. I participated in the interview at that time as the associate chief of staff for primary care. This evaluation resulted from a referral from the Drug Enforcement Administration (DEA) investigation due to the excessive number of opioid prescriptions the facility ordered and distributed. By that time, I became instrumental in applying opioid safety initiatives (OSI) beginning with education regarding the interpretation of urine drug screens. Our facility complied with urine drug screens; however, providers failed to interpret and take action on the results. For example, when there was no drug in the urine and there should have been drug in the urine, the prescribers continued dispensing opioid medications. The providers varied considerably in their prescribing practices when discovering presence of cannabinoids on the urine drug screen. Some considered marijuana to be an illicit substance just like cocaine, methamphetamine, and LSD; other providers looked the other way and continued to prescribe opioids for chronic pain.

As part of the National Pain Management, Opioid Safety Initiative committees, I reviewed a copious amount of educational materials on the subject. I distributed educational materials from the Opioid Safety Tool Kit Web site and lectures as our facility co-champion along with the pain psychologist.

Our facility was not originally part of the state Prescription Monitoring Program (PMP) in that the large health-care system did not report the opioids their providers were giving to the patients for community doctors to access as part of the state Prescription Monitoring Program. However, the community was a part of this program, and large health-care system providers were newly required to check the state PMP prior to ordering opiates for chronic pain and approximately yearly afterward. This was an unknown requirement for most of the primary care providers at this facility upon my arrival.

Some other providers were checking the Prescription Monitoring Program, but the majority were not. Later in the fall of 2016, the facility pharmacy did start reporting their opioid distribution to the state Prescription Monitoring Program. This was a giant leap forward for the community in that community providers could now monitor their patients on opioids for chronic pain who sought care at the large health-care system as well as in the community. Previously, the large health-care system employees were not able to check the state monitoring program because the general consensus was that monitoring patients would be a violation of the patients' rights. However, it became obvious that this was a vital safety requirement.

Unfortunately, senior leaders at this facility did not support primary care providers when they reported significant findings on the state Prescription Monitoring Program and other parameters for compliance with the safe use of opiates for chronic pain. To my surprise initially, patients who were found to be filling prescriptions at multiple community sites along with the large health-care system or did not have drug in the urine when they should have and their medications were appropriately stopped, instead of being embarrassed or ashamed that they were caught, the patients complained. Astonishingly, some of the patients reported feeling entitled to receive opioid medications even though they were not taking them or when they were receiving opioids from another facility. These patients complained to patient advocates, the chief of staff's office, the director's office, and to politicians. Patients' accounts of their situations regarding their opioid medications proved to be dishonest in many cases. Because physicians cannot disclose a patient's medical condition based upon the law, it is not easy to correct the misperceptions by nonclinical persons.

The internal inspectors conducted interviews which included the acting director, acting chief of staff, assistant director, associate director, associate chief of staff for primary care (me), and many others. Eventually, the inspection was suspended when the group determined that there was a rationale for increase in purchase of hydrocodone in the river state. Hydrocodone originally was a schedule III drug and became a schedule II drug in October 2014. In my experience, however, some of the providers had very poor prescribing habits which they attribute to pressure from the senior leadership prior to my arrival.

When my privileges were summarily suspended, I contacted the internal inspectors in the summer of 2017 to report my concern that in my absence, there would be nobody to support the primary care providers in the opioid safety initiatives which many of us implemented since my arrival in the fall of 2015. It was clear that a certain politician did not understand the importance of opioid safety as being more critical than voter satisfaction. She commanded the press, which published medically inaccurate articles stating that the patients had their medications stopped without being evaluated. These patients' statements grossly misrepresented the facts. The press failed to realize that providers potentially uncovered illegal acts by patients such as selling their medications in the community. Other patients increased their medication doses and used up their monthly allotment too quickly; consumed their medications inappropriately such as chewing fentanyl patches or snorting their crushed pills; and had medical diagnoses that put the patients using opioids at increased risk for heart arrhythmia, respiratory depression, overdose, and death. All of the patients were informed by the clinical primary care team or other clinical expert of why changes were needed in their treatment plan, and the communication was documented in the clinical electronic medical record.

Many of the physicians, pharmacists, social workers, mental health providers, medical leaders, and medical program assistants were well aware of opioid safety initiative implementation and the process changes occurring at our facility. The professionals endorsed the safety changes being made to prevent unintentional overdoses for our patients. We worked together as a team; but unfortunately, we were fighting uneducated nonclinical people in positions of power. The uneducated nonclinical people in positions of power chose to glorify their own names and status in exchange for the lives of people in the community, including our patients.

As a consequence resulting from the ignorant actions of the senior leaders, the facility lost good employees who felt like they lost the struggle in applying opioid safety at this facility. The clinical staff once had a strong leader (me) willing to advocate for righteousness at the expense of being publicly humiliated and defamed personally and professionally by uneducated nonclinical leaders in positions of power. To the employees' dismay, the compassionate activist (as I was addressed) became the facility scapegoat to appease politicians and left the large health-care system altogether. Primary care lost their associate chief of staff for primary care (me), administrative officer for primary care, medical outpatient clinic leader at a community clinic, nurse leader for the clinic, clerical leader for the clinic, and four other primary care providers within a six-week period of time following my departure. All of these employees left due to lack of support by the executive leadership team at this facility especially in regard to application of opioid safety initiatives. I say lack of support out of kindness. Truly, previous leaders bullied and pressured primary care providers to practice medicine in a manner that was against their own ethical standards. In contrast to the past, the providers appreciated the support they received by a strong advocate with integrity, willing to do the right things for the right reasons. Following my departure, the providers at the facility felt vulnerable once again.

CHAPTER 4

Welcome New Director

Woe unto them that are wise in their own
eyes, and prudent in their own sight!

—Isaiah 5:21, KJV

At the end of 2016, the facility welcomed a new director, a retired military leader. Leaders and other employees were given the opportunity to share what was most important to them for the new director to understand in relation to their service line. I, of course, said, "Please believe in the importance of opioid safety, and support the providers." This statement landed on deaf ears.

Soon after the new director's arrival, it became clear that he was all about numbers, all about data. He shouted this from the rooftops at every meeting, every special event, and every town hall. He was also all about the patients. This is an admirable quality; but in his clinical ignorance, he chose patient satisfaction over patient and community safety. This type of ignorance frightened me. I realized by the spring of 2017 that I could not support this leader. His narcissistic persona, clinical ignorance, dictatorship, top-down leadership style, and embarrassing delivery style soon created a hostile work environment for me. When the director announced that we were to add four overbooks a day to each provider and there was no negotiation, my heart broke. The director also continuously coerced the chief of staff to reinstate opioids to patients who were caught diverting opioids, doctor shopping around town for additional opioids, and abused their opioids. I continued to educate the executive leaders about opioid safety; but it was clear that they were not interested. The new director continuously reminded me that the he "will always believe the patients" when they complained, and they did complain.

I reported my concerns to my supervisor, the chief of staff. During a ninety-minute meeting with the chief of staff in the spring of 2017, I delivered my exit review. I outlined all of my concerns with supporting documentation present. I informed the chief of staff that I was considering reporting the director's actions to be creating a hostile work environment for me and that I could not support such a leader. I praised the work of my two administrative officers and advocated for their support in my absence. I told my supervisor that I would be seeking employment elsewhere at another facility within the health-care system. He expressed understanding stating, "Why I do believe I have tears in my eyes." I always thought he was a nice man. He just couldn't stand up to the director to support his service chiefs and providers. I lost the battle of overbooks for the providers. I knew some providers would leave from the burnout this would create *again*. I knew I was no longer effective as the ACOS for primary care. The director and chief of staff went behind my back, reinstating the practice of overbooking. We were so close to having a full primary care provider staff. I lost the battle. Not only did I lose the battle on overbooks; I soon lost the war on opioid safety.

I filled out applications for leadership positions on the company website. Within a few days, I interviewed for the chief of staff in another state by clinical video. I interviewed well, and they asked me for references. References were called the next day, and I knew I was leaving the river city. An amusing fact regarding reference checks was that the facility in another state contacted my best friend because she worked at the other facility in which I interviewed for chief of staff. These people were serious! I felt relief and excitement. Colleagues cautioned me about the history of that other facility and opioid use there. I replied that I would be of great help to the new facility in support of applying opioid safety initiatives.

The following week or two, the chief of staff from another facility on the east coast called me to tell me about a new leadership position they were developing as part of their system. He thought I would be perfect for the job, and he invited me for a site visit. My husband and I traveled to the east coast for the site visit. I accepted the position, and we found a house with a beautiful seaside landscape. I knew I would have to turn down the chief of staff position in the other state; but I hadn't heard much since all of the reference calls. The east coast position fit me like a glove. I would be working with the Osteopathic College, local hospitals, and politicians, networking to provide teaching opportunities and access to health care on the east coast.

CHAPTER 5

Undesired Attention and the Headlines

A faithful witness will not lie: but a false witness will utter lies.

—Proverbs 14:5, KJV

In late spring of 2017, a local newspaper published a very unflattering article. A politician is quoted, vilifying the facility in her own state and the large health-care system in general, based upon one-sided deceptive reports by patients. Many of the politicians contacted our facility on behalf of patients. This was standard practice. Primary care leadership reached out to the patients on behalf of the facility regarding opioid safety concerns. We were a knowledgeable team. We provided the written responses to the official inquiries. One politician, however, had been relentless. She continuously "over advocated for patients" not understanding their clinical history and ultimately coerced the executive leadership team of the facility, most notably the director (with no medical knowledge) and chief of staff to act upon inaccurate clinical reports. The chief of staff in turn often asked me for a chart review and recommendation; but with continued pressure by the politician and the director, both without medical knowledge, the chief of staff had been reported to approach primary care providers without my knowledge to "reconsider their opioid plan." Often, I was notified by these providers and/or pharmacists who filled the prescriptions that they felt coerced into doing something unsafe for the patients which could result in unintentional overdose and death.

Later in the spring of 2017, a news story aired featuring patients stating their opioids were "cut off" with no communication, and the politician ridiculed opioid safety efforts by the facility. The story also featured the chief of staff who made ill-informed comments about provider practices which I found surprising since he had been supportive of our opioid safety initiative (OSI) efforts all along, often being recognized along with the director for our OSI best practices. The medical charts contained documentation to prove why the opiates were stopped for safety of the interviewed patients. The politician, newscaster, and chief of staff failed to check facts prior to broadcasting the story. These facts, of course, may not be shared publicly due to HIPAA rules which was one of the reasons I declined the interview.

My name was used extensively in a derogatory manner during the telling of the news piece. As previously mentioned, my photograph, released without my permission by the director, violated policy. The feature displayed my photograph throughout the story.

As opioid safety provider champion for the facility and associate chief of staff for primary care with fifteen years of primary care, pain management, and opioid safety experience at the large health-care system, I would be the physician staff would turn to for advice. Chart review is a standardized practice for champions and associate chiefs of staff to use and involves reviewing the state Prescription Monitoring Program site medication list, opioid agreement, urine drug screen, pill counts, radiographs, provider note history, and other appropriate information. When the urine does not have the drug in the urine or the patient has been filling opiates in the community and at the large health-care system regularly, the opiate agreement (reviewed and signed by the patient previously) has been violated. It is standard practice and backed by state medical law not to renew opiates at the large health-care facility if the agreement is violated. The patients are informed by a primary team member of the findings in a respectful manner. Additional care is offered.

During the same time in late spring of 2017, my husband and I drove back from the east coast interview to our home by the river state. The chief of staff asked me to come back from my trip early to be interviewed by an investigative body. Clueless as to the reason for the interview, I agreed. I planned to report back to work at that time. While driving home from the east coast, my administrative officer texted me a link to the news story. I grew ill. There I was, my picture blasted everywhere during the report, the picture I never gave permission to release mind you, the picture that came from the director's assistant, the picture that was only to be used for another large health-care facility's promotion when the employee and I attended a promotional conference well over a year ago, and the picture that only the director could have released in the end without my permission. Big mistake! Big!

The patients were untruthful during the interview, and because of Health Insurance Portability and Accountability Act (HIPAA) of 1996, I cannot elaborate further. The reporter failed to check facts. The politician, mentioned in the report, failed to check facts. The chief of staff for the facility "threw me under the bus" according to everyone that watched the interview and failed to check facts. The only reason patients would not receive their opioids would be if they were caught diverting, found to be doctor shopping in the community by state pharmacy reporting, discovered to be clearly abusing their medications, or observed to have a health problem putting them at risk for overdose.

Communication to patients can be done by nursing staff, clinical pharmacy specialists, and providers assigned to cover for absent providers. Access for patients is a big deal as we all know. Why would anyone insist on using an appointment slot to see a patient face-to-face to tell him or her she was found to be getting opioids elsewhere, so we cannot give them at this facility? Why would a face-to-face visit be required to inform the patient that no opioid was found in the urine when he or she was filling 360 tabs of oxycodone monthly? This would be a waste of resources when a simple telephone call by a clinical staff member is the standard of care across the country. Somehow, the face-to-face requirement became the expectation, and according to the chief of staff, the nurse executive was the initiator of this requirement to protect the nursing staff from angry patients.

I get it in theory; but nursing staff is part of the whole primary care team and often the major communicators to patients as the standard of care. Sorry nurse executive!

After hearing the news story, I immediately sent the chief of staff on the east coast the news link to review. I did not want him to think I was running away from something. Well, actually I was running away from something, a bully of a director who obviously has a problem with a mature woman leader who was not afraid to support her staff. The director started at the facility at the end of 2016. I was excited to finally have a director for our facility, and I was sure that he would support opioid safety initiatives—wrong!

Opioid safety became my passion. For fifteen years at the large health-care system, I fought for the prevention of unintentional overdoses for our patients and our citizens. A pain psychologist and I were appointed as facility co-champions for opioid safety initiative (OSI) implementation. We became experts by necessity, at least as much "experts" as one could be without formal training, for me anyway.

I had experience. As I previously explained, I inherited a large panel of patients on opiates as a provider by the Great Lakes, and I and was in on the ground level of a multidisciplinary approach in dealing with pain patients. This facility is one of the best in the country now, and I was in at the ground level for eight years. The anesthesiologist and ACOS for primary care are still leading the cause by the Great Lakes, my former pain specialist and supervisor. I am proud of their accomplishments. The east coast chief of staff replied to me and expressed no concern about my dilemma, stating this is the way the media is with the large health-care system, no big deal. Whew!

After being on leave for two weeks, I returned to work at the Facility by the River in late spring 2017 as directed by the chief of staff. I attended an interview, along with others from leadership, conducted by an investigative body. Surprised to see my schedule that day, I questioned the chief of staff about the group's interest. He said it was no big deal and gave me some watered-down version of their interest in his usual politically savvy manner. I walked into a trap.

"Dr. Sky, will you please raise your right hand? Do you swear or affirm the testimony you're about to provide is the truth, the whole truth, and nothing but the truth?"

"I do. I swear."

The investigators asked a myriad of opioid safety initiative questions. I explained the state of affairs of the facility when I arrived. This facility lost sixteen primary care providers during a two-year period under previous leadership or lack thereof. Nine providers in one of the locations sought opportunities in specialty medicine, retired, took extended leave, or resigned. Three providers resigned from another location and an outpatient clinic. Four providers resigned yet another location. I am certain there may have been more losses that remain undiscovered.

One non-clinician and one physician interviewed me. The doctor was on the telephone, and the interview was recorded. They were following up on another governing body's report which I hadn't seen. I spent over an hour with the two interviewers and soon realized I was probably the target. We reviewed the same outpatient clinic information that I reviewed previously with other investigating offices. One of our campuses included multiple outpatient clinics which were known to have opioid-prescribing outliers nationally in the number of opioid pills prescribed.

I have since reviewed the Ignorant Oversight Body (IOB) report and the chief of staff's testimony to the Accountability Office to the IOB. His testimony contained lies, lies, and more lies. His lies did not always include me either. The chief of staff lied under oath about the reason a provider left the facility. He lied under oath about another physician's performance. He lied about disciplining me about opioid safety practices. When one of the interviewers asked the chief of staff for proof, he stated he could not find any proof in his files. Duh! That is because the disciplinary encounter never occurred! I was praised, not disciplined. I served as the facility's opioid safety initiative champion prescriber. I supported the primary care staff and the pharmacists who did not want to fill prescriptions for known diverters, doctor shoppers, and unfortunate addicts when they tried to circumvent our system using community care. This same chief of staff supported our efforts, often publicly recognized by the regional supervising office and others for our efforts. Talk about straddling the fence. I now don't understand how the man can sleep at night. Other leaders expressed concern about the chief of staff and his so-called "memory problem." In all fairness, I previously believed he was either too busy to remember conversations and action items or having early dementia problems. I gave him the benefit of the doubt. Unfortunately, his testimony completely convinced me that he is simply an untruthful politician type of puppet trying to please a dictator of a director who is pulling his strings.

The interview by the Accountability Office to the Ignorant Oversight Body (AO-IOB) went well in my opinion. The interviewers asked me for proof of my statements adding that "everyone says they have proof, but we rarely see it in the end." I bombarded the two interviewers with proof over a two-week period of time. I worked on sending proof full time. I don't think they will be that flip with an interviewee in the future. I doubt they had enough time to look through everything I sent.

My most astonishing memory of the interview was when the interviewers queried about disciplinary actions taken by the chief of staff. I asked who this was in regard to, and they laughed and said me. Me? Are you kidding? I was rewarded for my efforts. Just two weeks prior to this interview, I received a fully successful rating on my review, the highest rating. Six months prior, I received an outstanding proficiency rating citing opioid safety initiatives and other leadership accomplishments. The chief of staff conferred with me regularly about opioid safety cases. Pharmacists, mental health providers, emergency department providers, primary care providers, social workers, nursing staff, and others consulted with me regularly about opioid safety questions and concerns. Questioning my performance remains the greatest surprise and puzzling question asked by the interviewers. The two men had a sidebar conversation in my presence following my reply and asked me for proof. One of the first documents I sent them was the review I just received two weeks prior along with my 2016 outstanding proficiency.

I couldn't believe the chief of staff fabricated his testimony. He committed perjury! I knew him to be a weak leader; but I did not know him to be dishonest. I thought to myself that I must have misunderstood something.

In summary, one day I returned to work from leave, and the following day, I received a summary suspension of privileges citing aspects of my practice "do not meet the accepted standards of practice and constitute an imminent threat to patient welfare." I understand the director ordered the chief of staff to recommend an immediate summary suspension of privileges in response to public embarrassment and political pressure, abusing his authority as director. The chief of staff agreed and issued the summary suspension of privileges, abusing his authority as the chief of staff. Issuing a summary suspension of privileges is warranted only when "sufficient evidence exists, based on the preliminary fact finding, that a practitioner may have demonstrated substandard care, professional misconduct or patient care." The director and chief of staff failed to follow procedures and processes located in the Medical Staff Bylaws and policy pertaining to credentialing and privileging. Actions by the director and chief of staff were carried out in haste and retaliatory in nature in response to public embarrassment and political pressure.

Primary care providers at this facility presently do not have a supportive leader or opioid safety initiative champion provider to consult regarding opioid safety concerns. Several of the strong ethical providers, unwilling to be coerced by the director and chief of staff, have since been targeted for removal from employment. One strong ethical provider at our contract site was recently given an offer of employment by this facility by the river. Senior leadership rescinded the offer during my summary suspension of privileges, again reflecting the political environment and abuse of authority by leaders previously mentioned. The physician is a highly respected leader in his community.

Many of the service line leaders and chiefs reported concerns that their privileges and employment may be terminated at the whim and abuse of the authority of a director and chief of staff succumbing to public embarrassment and political pressure.

Lastly, there is a substantial danger to public health and safety if the large health-care system and the community fail to initiate and uphold opioid safety measures. Leaders, political representatives, and others have the right to inquire about their patients' and citizens' concerns. Medical concerns are routinely investigated and communicated to the patient and office submitting the inquiry as part of our daily work in the primary care administrative office. The leaders, political representatives, and others do not have the right to abuse their positions of authority and coerce physicians to prescribe or treat patients when the providers know their recommendations may result in iatrogenic harm to the patient including unintentional overdose and death related to opioid prescribing. Nonclinical leaders, political representatives, and others do not know the clinical background of the patients and citizens they serve. Clinicians know the clinical history of the patients and citizens they serve. Leaders, political representatives, and others do not have the right to abuse their positions of authority to suspend a provider's privileges, rescind employment offers, or threaten termination of an employee based upon misleading reports.

One of the facility's hospital locations is in a city known to have the highest rate of unintentional overdose rates in the state and is one of the highest across the country. We owe it to our patients and community citizens to prevent unintentional overdoses and risk of death related to opioids. The Centers for Disease Control Guideline for Prescribing Opioids for Chronic Pain is our major source for OSI guidance and goals as a nation. The large health-care system officials put out a Memorandum in the winter of 2014, with the subject titled: Opioid Safety Initiative Updates with goals and guidance. The large health-care system has an opioid safety toolkit to use for guidance with a multitude of resources. These professional clinical references and others have been used extensively over the past eighteen months at this facility under primary care and OSI champion leadership in collaboration with other service line leaders, clinical pharmacy specialists, pain psychology champions, and others in full support by the chief of staff until recently.

CHAPTER 6

Fighting the Summary Suspension of Privileges

That no man go beyond and defraud his brother in any
matter: because that the LORD is the avenger of all such,
as we also have forewarned you and testified. For God hath
not called us unto uncleanness, but unto holiness.

—1 Thessalonians 4:6, 7, KJV

I will be forever grateful to one of my colleagues. Following my receipt of the summary suspension, I immediately shared the letter with my friend. This devastated her. I learned the following week that she almost submitted her resignation the next work day. Instead, knowing she had the security to resign at any time without consequences, she decided to stay to support me and the other chiefs. It bothered my friend that I was slapped with a summary suspension after two and one-half weeks of leave. She advised me to seek sophisticated legal representation to protect my professional reputation and personal reputation. She understood that patients spoke out publicly on the news; but I had the documentation to prove why opioids were stopped for safety and that I could not disclose medical information. Embarrassed, the director reacted in a knee-jerk reaction, retaliated, and used me as a scapegoat in retaliation for embarrassing the facility.

My colleague suggested that I put together a time line of important dates from when I came to the present with major events such as the peer review meeting where I announced that I was stepping down from being opioid safety initiative prescribing champion. This never stuck. I was still the OSI prescribing champion. Nobody wanted to accept my resignation, and I went back to fighting the opioid epidemic.

My colleague reminded me of the redundancy I put into our system's tapering process which included assistance by primary care team nurses, covering providers, doc of the day, clinical pharmacy specialist assistance, and primary care leadership support. She encouraged me to find out how other facilities within the large health-care system address similar challenges and what is their reasonable standard of care.

I followed my friend's advice. I learned I was not alone in the fight against the opioid epidemic as a primary care leader. Other facilities fought the same fight. Many facilities face primary care provider turnover challenges and limited coverage. The primary care leader ends up filling in the gap, just like me. Other facilities had solid coverage plans, but this was not the norm.

Realizing I needed to clear my name first and then go after the people that acted unfairly, the need to retain legal counsel became clear. My character had been defamed publicly. My work environment was nothing short of hostile. I could not find other employment within the large health-care system, and I could not return to my job at that facility under the current leadership.

I was given names and numbers of attorneys to contact with solid reputations. I contacted three attorneys. None of them had experience with the large health-care system. One stated he would learn the system and to call him if I couldn't find anyone with experience. This search for solid representation became challenging. I searched for qualified attorneys and found two firms. One contacted me first, and I retained an attorney with a $5,000.00 retainer. This was not going to be cheap.

I sent documentation to my attorney which included our facility's medical bylaws and policy. I sent a multitude of supporting evidence including my recent glowing midterm performance review, my outstanding proficiency from 2016, e-mails showing support of my efforts from my supervisor, the chief of staff, and other documents reflecting my efforts as the primary care ACOS.

My attorney wrote an impressive letter of response to the chief of staff. Brilliant! The money spent proved to be worth the sting in my pocketbook. The letter is redacted in an attempt to maintain confidentiality.

COS
address
Via email and Certified Mail

Dear Dr. COS,

This Law Group represents the interests of Dr. Sky in all proceedings related to the automatic suspension of health care privileges with your facility. The notice to Dr. Sky was dated Spring 2017. On behalf of Dr. Sky, this letter serves as her written response to the allegations.

I. Allegation: Failure to implement opioid safety initiatives with patients in a safe and ethical manner.

II. Standard for Immediate Summary Suspension: Immediate action must be taken in the best interest of patient care due to the potential of **imminent danger** to the health and well-being of an individual. Bylaws §. Failure to take action will result in an imminent danger to the safety and welfare of an individual. Bylaws § (Emphasis added.)

III. Standard for Implementing Review Process: **Sufficient evidence exists**, based on the preliminary fact finding, that a practitioner may have demonstrated **substandard care**, professional **misconduct**, or professional **incompetence** that impacts the practitioner's ability to deliver safe, high quality patient care. Bylaws §.

IV. Response:

A. The allegation does not reflect grounds for summary suspension or further investigation.

The suspension notice alleges a failure to implement opioid safety initiatives in a safe and ethical manner. Dr. Sky, as Associate Chief of Staff for primary care providers and Opioid Safety Initiative Co-Champion, was instrumental in implementing processes and procedures for opioid prescribing. COS was an active participant throughout this process.

The allegation refers to an unsatisfactory facility *policy*. The allegation has nothing to do with a threat of an unsafe *practitioner*. Immediate action, if anything, should have involved a change in facility policies and practices. If revisions to any policies should be made, they should be made in accordance with sound medical practice, and in compliance with federal and state laws and regulations, appropriate ethical standards, as well as the recent safety initiative of Gov. River. *However, a physician disciplinary proceeding is not the appropriate platform to address such matters.*

If indeed the bylaws were followed and the Chief of Staff recommended summary suspension to the Director, such actions constituted overreach and an abuse of discretion on the part of both of these individuals, as the allegation cannot form the basis for summary suspension. Bylaws §§.

B. There is no evidence to indicate that Dr. Sky demonstrated substandard care, professional misconduct, or professional incompetence in her clinical practice.

No specific allegations accompany the notice to Dr. Sky. However, this response will discuss recent patient care at OC facility. This discussion will not address patient satisfaction issues such as chart flags, or any other matter not directly related to the potential of imminent danger to the health and well-being of an individual.

Dr. Sky, as the facility pain provider champion, responded to many opioid chart review requests. Also, as Associate Chief of Staff for primary care providers, she also covered duty for multiple providers. Certain patients at this facility received communication, with thorough explanation, about plans to taper medications, where clinically appropriate.

When conducting opioid chart review requests, or covering clinical duties for another provider, Dr. Sky made certain decisions regarding prescription refills for patients.

If Dr. Sky determined that it was appropriate to taper or discontinue medications, she did so based-upon sound practices, including the following examples:

1. Nobody took medications out of the patients' hands. Rather, the patients would receive a phone call after Dr. Sky's chart review and would be told of the recommendation to discontinue or change medications due to safety concerns.

2. The patient was invited to come to the facility for a face-to-face visit where the patient's needs could be addressed, which could usually be accommodated on a same-day walk-in, or next day basis.

3. Pain management, physiatry, physical therapy, or alternative treatments such as chiropractic care or acupuncture were offered. Comfort kits were available.

4. Along with chart review, prescription drug monitoring program records were obtained and reviewed. All active medications, prescribed dosages, combinations of medications, as well as patient histories, were reviewed for contraindications and other safety risks.

5. If medications were contraindicated (e.g. opioid and benzodiazepine combinations; opiates for patients with obstructive sleep apnea), the patient would be informed of the need to discontinue or taper certain of the medications. This was due to safety, ethical, and liability concerns.

6. Unusually high doses were sometimes tapered because of safety concerns such as the need to avoid risk of unintentional overdose. The Clinical Pharmacy Specialist was consulted for taper schedules.

7. Negative drug screens did not require tapering. Negative drug screens mean that a patient is not ingesting the medications, and is probably diverting their prescription medications.

8. If the patient obtained multiple prescriptions from different providers for the same controlled substances, additional prescriptions for that medication would not be authorized.

These decisions were part of the opioid chart review and diligent oversight of the prescribing practices of the facility. It was Dr. Sky's responsibility in the role of Associate Chief of Staff for primary care providers and Opioid Safety Initiative Co-Champion to take these actions. Under no circumstances could Dr. Sky be expected to rubber-stamp a plan of care involving Schedule II controlled substances where patient safety concerns were present, or where diversion was highly likely. To do so would be in violation of medical ethics, standards of care, and, in some cases, the law. Contrary to local media hype, no patients were cut-off "cold turkey." No patients suffered physical harm.

C. Legal and ethical compliance.

Dr. Sky's legal duties include compliance with the following laws.

a. 21 U.S. Code § 841(a): it is a felony offense to dispense a controlled substance outside the scope of professional practice and not for a legitimate medical purpose. 21 U.S. Code § 802 (10) defines the term "dispense" to include prescribe.

b. 21 C.F.R. 1306.04: to be valid, a prescription for a controlled substance must be issued for a legitimate medical purpose by a practitioner acting in the usual course of professional practice.

Physicians are disciplined by state medical boards, have DEA registrations revoked, and are charged with crimes every day for participating in "pill mill" prescribing practices. Tell-tale evidence of wrongdoing includes prescribing when a patient's urine drug screen is negative, and prescribing even when the patient obtains multiple prescriptions from multiple providers. Additionally, a recipe for malpractice and additional medical board sanctions involves prescribing in a manner that is contraindicated, thereby placing the patient at risk for serious physical harm or death. Dr. Sky's practices protected both the practitioners of the facility, and the health and safety of the patients.

Hippocratic ethical values apply to the ethics of prescribing medications. "[A]citing in patients' best interest is relevant to opioid treatment decisions since it requires physicians to deny inappropriate treatments requested by patients, no matter how much patients or their advocates want that treatment." Ballantyne JC, Fleisher LA. *Ethical issues in opioid prescribing for chronic pain*. Pain. 2010;148(3):365-367. Additionally, the AMA Code of Ethics states that patients have the right:

To receive information from their physicians and to have opportunity to discuss the benefits, risks, and costs of appropriate treatment alternatives, including the risks, benefits and costs of forgoing treatment. Patients should be able to expect that their physicians will provide guidance about what they consider the optimal course of action for the patient based on the physician's objective professional judgment.

AMA Principles of Medical Ethics 1.1.3(b). Dr. Sky's practices were aligned with this principal. She acted in her best objective clinical judgment in deciding optimal courses of action, ensured that her concerns were communicated to the patients and that the patients were invited to be seen for an office visit to discuss concerns and changes.

D. Conclusion.

Due to the lack of evidence of either potential or imminent danger to the health and well-being of any individuals, a summary suspension cannot continue, and Dr. Sky hereby requests that her privileges be reinstated, and *that no further review be taken.* Bylaws § 9.01(3)(a). Furthermore, a review process is warranted only when "sufficient evidence exists, based on the preliminary fact finding, that a practitioner may have demonstrated substandard care, professional misconduct or professional incompetence that impacts the practitioner's ability to deliver safe, high quality patient care." Bylaws § 9.01(4)(a). Should a review process go forward notwithstanding the insufficiency of the evidence, Dr. Sky requests that the Medical Center Director reinstate her privileges pending the outcome of the clinical review, in accordance with Bylaws §.

Very Truly Yours,
Law Group

The human resource chief tried to conclude the summary suspension proposal in a timely manner to prevent reporting me to the National Practitioner Data Bank (NPDB), knowing the proposal was unfair. However, I learned from the law group that this should not be done, and I received the following documentation to submit. Stressed, I pressed on. My attorney supplied me with the following letter. Again, I was grateful for the support even though it was costly.

Regarding: NPDB be reporting of summary suspension

> Dear Dr. Sky,
> This letter will serve to address your concerns regarding the hospital's obligation to report your summary suspension to the National Practitioner Data Base (NPDB). The summary suspension should not be reported unless final adverse actions are taken. I spoke with the facil-

ity Council today by telephone and she stated her agreement with my conclusion.

Reporting obligations for the large healthcare system are different than for other eligible entities under the NPDB rules. The large healthcare system reports to the NPDB under a memorandum of understanding that generally governs reporting, rather than a NPDB guidebook C, and PDB guidebook, B–3. Therefore, we must turn to the policy. Specific to the summary suspension process, the reporting Policy (1) (6) (1) (3) ©:

Adverse professional review action.

Any final professional review action that adversely affects the clinical privileges upper practitioner for a period longer than 30 days, including the surrender her clinical privileges or any voluntary restriction of such privileges, while the physician or dentist is under investigation, it is reportable to the and PDB pursuant to the provisions of the BHA policy regarding an PDB reporting policy

Policy (1) (6) (7) further clarifies: If a final action is taken, based on professional competence or professional conduct grounds, both the summary suspension, if greater than 30 days, and the final action will be reported to the NPDB are Policy section (9) (A) (1) dates:

When the Medical Center Director renders a final determination based on a clinical professional review, relating to possible incompetence or improper professional conduct, that adversely affects the clinical privilege of a physician or dentist by reducing, restricting, suspending, revoking, or failing to renew such privileges for a period longer than 30 days, such action must be reported.

There is no doubt the facility should not report summary suspension to the NPDB unless final adverse action is taken affecting her clinical privileges. As I stated above, facility Council concurs with my conclusions.

As always, if you have any questions or concerns do not hesitate to contact me.

Very truly yours,
Law Group

My privileges were reinstated without findings in the early summer of 2017, removed again three days later by the director, and then finally reinstated for a second time a couple of weeks later. What a rollercoaster ride!

CHAPTER 7

Where Is the Support from Leadership?

> If a man say, I love God, and hateth his brother, he is
> a liar; for he that loveth not his brother whom he hath
> seen, how can he love God whom he hath not seen?
>
> —1 John 4:20, KJV

The chief of staff failed to attend opioid safety initiative workgroup meetings as our leader. I took over as the leader with a pain psychologist in the chief of staff's absence. I put together agendas, and the group remained somewhat active. Eventually, the pain psychologist and I were officially appointed as co-chairs for opioid safety initiative for our facility and Regional Pain Management Workgroup. The psychologist attended these meetings and reported to our facility because I had a conflict with the Professional Standards Board/Clinical Executive Board meetings which could not be changed. In every other way, I became our facility's opioid-prescribing expert and primary educator.

I began educating primary care providers on how to interpret urine drug screen results. Providers were ordering urine drug screens, but they did not act on the results. They did not understand the results. I educated the primary care staff continuously as a group and individually. This education expanded to the emergency department physicians, mental health providers, social workers, and hospitalists. The psychologist and I spent over six hours educating the patient advocates. Despite all of this time and education, the advocates sided with the patients every time. The advocates would bring patients directly to the providers' offices interrupting patient care for other patients. The advocates continuously called the primary care providers, nursing staff, primary care leadership, and others to try to get opioids reinstated on patients who were selling their medications in the community, doctor shopping at up to seventeen different locations, or found to be abusing their opioids by chewing their fentanyl patches or snorting crushed oxycodone or found to have overdosed on their opioids. Other patients were prescribed high pill counts of methadone with deadly cardiac arrhythmia potentials on their EKGs, use of oxygen for severe chronic obstructive pulmonary disease, severe obstructive sleep apnea and not using their CPAP machines, and other medical conditions which put them at high risk for respiratory depression and death. These prescribers were educated and monitored. Often, filling in for providers proved to be helpful in identifying unsafe practices.

When I approached these providers about their concerning prescribing practices, they often disclosed that they felt obligated to continue the unsafe practices because of visits or calls from the chief of staff at the time who told them, "Doctors are a dime a dozen...if you don't like it, you don't have to stay." I rehired a primary care provider who told me he heard I was supportive, so he wanted to come back to the facility. I asked him why he left initially, and he described the exit of many of the primary care providers, and he was stuck signing all of the opioid prescriptions. He tried to change the system and stuck it out for several months until he realized this practice was not going to change anytime soon. This provider did not come back in the end after television news story hit, and I believe he learned of my retirement from a close facility employee. I wished him well.

CHAPTER 8

Politician Is a Bad Word

These things I have spoken unto you, that in me ye
might have peace. In the world ye shall have tribulation;
but be of good cheer; I have overcome the world.

—John 16:33, KJV

This leads me to politicians and the large health-care system. Oh, my word, the power and influence politicians have on our health-care system. For years, my administrative staff and I have been answering what we call "political inquiries." In review, many patients write to their politicians often about anything and everything. This is not a bad practice. A political office by the Great Lakes area helped me get my GI Bill educational benefits to be honored when I encountered red tape in the past. This proved to be extremely helpful to me personally, and my gratitude to that politician will never end. As far as health care goes in the large health-care system and these inquiries, our administrative staff routinely contacts the patient about the issue and offers assistance in any way possible. Our administrative staff then writes a letter about the patient contact, and the inquiry is closed. For fifteen years, I participated in these political inquiries either as a physician or administrative leader. Until I accepted the position at this facility, the process seemed to work.

This facility's executive leadership team consisted of one leader who feared political inquiries, enough to make poor decisions in some instances. She was not too much of a clinical interference until the new director arrived in late 2016. We had strong acting directors prior to the new director's arrival. Political representatives would contact the leaders, and the leaders would meet or supply a written response to their questions. When the opioid safety initiative inquiries popped up, I was often consulted by a member of the executive leadership team for an informed response. Our primary care team presented weekly to the executives, using PowerPoint presentations, data, graphs, and other documents to educate the staff on primary care issues. The leaders were mostly interested in access. Opioid use for chronic pain takes up many appointments due to laws requiring frequent visits for use of opioid chronically. Opioid overdoses became a constant newspaper story and television news flash. Radio, television, newspapers, and public meetings flooded the public's awareness to this epidemic. I began sneaking in this topic at morning report, relating it to the all-important topic of access. I tend to disagree in that both are topics of major concern clinically. I have the PowerPoint presentations to prove all of our attempts to educate the executive leadership team on opioid safety concerns within our facility and community. Eventually, the chief of staff publicly shushed me during my presentation. I responded by asking to respectfully be permitted to finish my presentation. I finished my presentation.

Soon afterward, our administrative officer (AO) for primary care put together PowerPoint presentations to the executive leadership team centered around, you guessed it, opioid safety and access. I appreciated his boldness, especially since I had previously been publicly humiliated. This did not impede him. In fact, our administrative officer experienced more encounters and education centered around opioid safety than he ever imagined or wanted. The man was amazing with patients. He had the patience of Job, the highest compliment I could give. He's no pushover either. The administrative officer grasped the opioid safety matter and navigated patients' charts easily. He and I often educated the chief of staff about realities centered around patients' complaints. The chief of staff repeatedly overlooked documentation related to clinicians informing patients about their treatment plans and other important documentation supporting clinicians' treatment decisions. The chief of staff believed untruthful patients and reversed decisions by primary care providers, resulting in potential harm to patients or community members. Other times, he would call or approach a primary care provider (PCP) requesting him or her to "reconsider" the treatment plan. I would receive a telephone call from the PCP and confront the chief of staff, often showing him where to find information in the clinical chart. The chief of staff rarely met with the patients face-to-face to review treatment plans or make clinical recommendations. I would not expect him to; but when the chief of staff made it an impossible requirement for others to meet face-to-face with patients for all treatment plans, I expected him to do the same. This was a ridiculous requirement and physically, geographically, feasibly, and plausibly *impossible*. Clinicians understand this fact. Thus, I no longer consider the chief of staff to be a clinician. I consider the chief of staff a politician.

The word *politician* became a bad word when I started dealing with a certain politician. She's chimed in on medical issues as well and spearheaded attacks on the large health-care system for years. In 2016, she wrote about how badly the facility performed in applying opioid safety. The next year, her position on the topic changed completely, and now we are "cutting patients off at the knees." The problem with this woman is that she fails to check facts. She believes untruthful patients' stories and coerces executive leaders to reinstate opioids to diverters, doctor shoppers, addicts, and medically sick patients when opioids are contraindicated. The politician took two unfortunate patients who were addicted to opioids under her wing, acted inappropriately making treatment plan recommendations without a medical license, and coerced a ladder-climbing director to change medical plans on the two patients we were trying to help with their addiction problems. The politician and the director do not have medical degrees. The director, who is not a clinician, then coerced the chief of staff to change the treatment plans of these two patients, and the politician that the chief of staff has become approached primary care providers asking for reconsideration of treatment plans. In one clear-cut case, the chief of staff demanded the reinstatement of opioids to be prescribed by a primary care provider who documented his disagreement in the electronic medical record. This type of demand is illegal. This string of coercion is illegal. The politician, director, and chief of staff minimally violated medical laws prohibiting providers to prescribe under situations of unexpected urine drug screens, failure to present for appointments, violation of opioid agreements, known addiction, doctor shopping as found on state prescription monitoring programs, and more. Providers have lost their licenses for doing anything less. Unfortunately, at the large health-care system, politicians simply have too much power; *power* to act like doctors and dictate treatment plans; *power* to influence the Ignorant Oversight Body; *power* to influence directors, chiefs of staff, physicians, nurses, and other clinicians; *power* to influence the news media; *power* to influence leaders of the large health-care system; and *power* to influence the president? We shall see.

I retired in the fall of 2017 just short of twenty years of service because I had no other choice. No other facility within the system would hire me after the news report hit. Another facility hired me prior to the television news story; but that promotion fell through due to actions set into action by the politician, director, and chief of staff. My privileges were summarily suspended twice by the director and chief of staff. I later found the letter written to a prominent leader of the large health-care system demanding this action. When my charts were all medically reviewed internally and later externally, my privileges were reinstated. I was found to be clinically sound in my actions and recommendations, *twice*. I really would like to write to the president demanding action regarding the politician who appears to be practicing medicine; but I refrain.

"A soft answer turneth away wrath: but grievous words stir up anger"

—Proverbs 15:1, KJV

A few weeks later, I received a proposal for reprimand citing the same issues in which I had just been cleared citing policy violation. The perplexing detail was in reality, the chief of staff should have initiated opioid safety initiatives based upon the little weak policy we had in place two years prior to my arrival! There really was no true policy regarding face-to-face visits for making changes in patient treatment plans. The so-called "policy" requiring the face-to-face visit expectation came from the nurse executive because nursing staff complained to the primary care nurse manager. These two nursing leaders, the nurse executive and primary care nurse manager, commute together regularly to different campuses. The chief of staff disclosed that the nursing staff wanted the provider to take on all of the opioid safety discussions with patients during a conversation with another primary care provider and me. The primary care provider wanted to see all of the patients face-to-face to make changes in opioids; but she found this impossible to do because of the number of patients on opioids she inherited upon her arrival. She reported that seventy-five patients still needed to be seen for the month, and there were no appointments available. Again, with the number of patients on opioids, it was physically, mathematically, feasibly impossible to accomplish face-to-face visits by PC providers with all of the patients. Teamwork was needed. Phone call communication was essential and actually encouraged whenever possible for years by the large health-care system and privately in the community to increase access to primary care in a country with a shortage of primary care providers. The pain Medical Home Roadmap guidance from the large health-care system stresses the importance of teamwork with patient communication and specifically recommends nursing or social worker involvement.

CHAPTER 9

Fighting Back: Equal Rights Organization (ERO)

The fear of the LORD is to hate evil: pride, and arrogancy,
and the evil way, and the forward mouth, do I hate.

—Proverbs 8:13, KJV

My privileges were summarily suspended in the spring of 2017 following a leadership meeting led by our new director who started at the facility as part of the large health-care system at the end of 2016. The administrative officer of the director pulled me aside just prior to the meeting to inform me that the meeting was about the news program. I asked if I should leave. She said it was up to me. I stayed. The director said a lot about nothing. "We will get through this," "We need to clean out our closets," "Wipe away the cobwebs." What was he talking about? The director asked for questions. Silence. I raised my hand at the exact moment the director began speaking again. He barked, "Let me finish!" Embarrassed, I stayed silent, no doubt turning red, fair-skinned Irish in me. Eventually, I was able to speak, and I apologized for interrupting the director. I gazed directly at the director and said, "Respectfully sir, you did ask for questions, and I have one." I turned around to my colleagues and asked, "Does anyone have any questions for me? I feel like the elephant in the room. Actually, I am the elephant in the room." I smiled. The director barked again, "Big, that is inappropriate!" I replied, "Oh I'm sorry. I just wanted everyone to know why I did not participate in the interview. I would have had to speak poorly about the condition of the facility upon my arrival or disclose patient information, and we all know this would not be appropriate. Thank you for listening." I sat down. The director concluded the meeting. Puzzled faces were everywhere. Many had no idea what just happened. I skulked back to my office.

The chaplain appeared at my office door. He asked if he could do anything to help. Tears streamed down my face. I felt humiliated in front of my peers *again*. He left his cell number for me to use anytime. I carried his number with me everywhere, just in case. Colleagues texted, stopped by, called, and e-mailed messages of support. It was obvious to others that the director's behavior was anything but respectful or supportive. I felt broken.

Three hours later, the chief of staff appeared. I failed to notice the brown folder he carried with him and tucked away out of sight. More political speech, lots of fancy words without content or meaning, repetitive justification of actions to follow, lies. The folder appeared in plain sight. I knew what was coming next, or did I? More politics. I asked the chief of staff to please speak plainly and truthfully to me. I said I did not appreciate the political explanations. Bottom line, my privileges were summarily suspended. The letter cited, "Concerns have been raised to suggest that aspects of (my) clinical practice do not meet the accepted standards of practice and potentially constitute an imminent threat to patient welfare." Additionally, the allegation stated, "Failure to implement opioid safety initiative with patients in a safe and ethical manner." This action was serious and ridiculous at the same time, incongruent, perplexing, and retaliatory. It was late Friday afternoon on a holiday weekend. There was nothing I could do but wait until Tuesday to address this preposterous act ordered by the director and agreed upon by the chief of staff. I notified the chief of staff on the east coast and future boss about the letter. Amazingly enough, he was still supportive.

I informed the chief of staff that I had no choice but to file formal reports. We both knew the actions he and the director were executing were seriously wrong. It was clear that I was to take the fall and for what? A pushy politician's demands? A ladder-climbing director's pursuit of prestige? A weak chief of staff's inability to support his medical staff?

I contacted the facility ERO officer to explore my options regarding reporting a hostile work environment and wrongful suspension of privileges. He explained my options, and the report was filed. I contacted both the Equal Rights Organization and Hassle Free Office. The director had been publicly humiliating me regularly at this point, and I believe being an older female leader (successful one at that) really bothered him. I believe he felt threatened by my popularity which is what other leaders shared with me. The director developed a reputation of having his inexperienced comrades around him, calling the shots to experienced service line leaders. This frustrated us and slowed down our work. The director came to large health-care system from the military where he was allegedly charged with harassing a female leader, at least according to the local newspaper upon his arrival. I learned not to trust this newspaper personally, so I take this finding as an alleged charge in all fairness to the director.

The suspension of my privileges was a different story. The facility's executives failed to follow the medical staff bylaws in that they did not follow the process for this action. They did not meet with the Professional Standards Board (PSB) and did not allow me to speak to the PSB prior to the action. They did not meet with the Clinical Executive Board (CEB) and did not allow me to speak to the CEB prior to the action. Their action affected a condition of my employment which justified ERO discrimination according to one of the oversight counselors. I lost a promotional opportunity which is something I lost as a condition of employment which also justified ERO discrimination. I filed a formal complaint with the ERO office.

The ERO process is cumbersome. I filed my complaint in the spring of 2017. After speaking with an ERO counselor, my case went forward officially. Parties were interviewed on both sides. My case was considered to be justified to be considered as serious harassment and elevated to the investigation phase in the winter of 2017. This was my redacted response to the investigative board should I have moved forward:

COMPLAINANTS' AFFIDAVIT

I, **Dr. Big Sky** am an __Employee of ___ applicant to _x_ former employee of
The Large Health-care System:
(Agency) Large Health Care Facility
(Office) River Facility
Located at: The River City
In the capacity of: Associate Chief of Staff for Primary Care
My telephone number during working hours is: xxx

I HAVE BEEN ADVISED OF THE FOLLOWING:

I am required by regulations and Large Health Care System policy to cooperate fully and promptly with the investigator who has been assigned to conduct a thorough and impartial investigation into a complaint of discrimination against the Large Health Care System. I must provide a statement for the investigative report which is true and complete to the best of my knowledge and which discloses all of my firsthand knowledge having a bearing on the merits of the complaint. My statement is provided under oath (or affirmation), without a pledge of confidentiality, in accordance with Equal Rights Organization Commission rules and regulations and Large Health Care System policy. This means that any employee(s) whom I accuse of discrimination or other acts of impropriety may be shown relevant portions of my affidavit and be provided an opportunity to respond for the record. In addition, the complainant and the appropriate Departmental officials involved in the ERO complaint process will receive the entire investigative file. I have the right to review my statement prior to signing it and may make initialized corrections if it is incomplete or inaccurate. I have the right to receive a copy of the signed statement.

COMPLAINANT:
Background Questions

1. What are your name, job title?

    Dr. Big Sky, Associate Chief of Staff for Primary Care

2. Do you have a representative? If yes, what is that person's name, address, city and state and contact information?

    Mr. Attorney

3. Please identify the city and state where you are employed?

    The River City, Retired as of the fall of 2017,

4. How long have you worked for the Large Health Care System?

    15 years

5. How long have you worked in your current position?

    2 years

6. At the time of the incidents noted in these claims, what was your position?

    Associate Chief of Staff for Primary Care

7. How long have you worked for the Organization?

    Over 19 years

8. Who is your first line supervisor? What is his/her title?

    Dr. Chief of Staff

9. How long have you been under his/her supervision?

    2 years

10. Please state your age, month and year of birth?

    Early retirement age

11. Please state your sex?

    Female

12. Did you received training in the agency's protocol procedures for employees to report harassment? If so, when?

    Yes, yearly

Whether complainant was subjected to a hostile work environment based on sex (female) and age as evidenced by the following events:

Claim# 1. During the winter of 2017, complainant endured 30 to 45 minutes of ridicule, harassment and personal humiliation from angry patients while the Director, stood by and smiled. The Director stated to the complainant, "I will always believe the patients."

1. During the winter of 2017, where did this incident occur with the angry patients and Mr. Director?

    Auditorium, Building 10, FBTR

2. Why were the angry patients upset?

    One patient was upset that his compensation and pension outcome was not as he wanted and he directed his comments at the administrative officer to the deputy chief of staff and leader of Compensation and Pension. She is a black female, and I believe close to my age. Mr. Director allowed this patient to direct angry comments to the group focusing on Ms. AO while Mr. Director stood up front as the host and smiled.

    Another patient identified me publicly and complained about opioids and how I was responsible for his pain and suffering while Mr. Director stood up front as the host and smiled.

3. Who was present during this incident by name, title?

Leaders of the facility as part of Leadership training.

Dr. Associate Chief of Staff for Acute Medicine; Mr. Administrative Officer1 for Primary Care; Mr. Administrative Officer for Acute Medicine; Ms. Chief of Mental Health; Ms. Nurse Manager Mental Health; Chaplain; Mr. HR Chief, Mr. Director; Ms. AO to the Director; Dr. Chief of Staff

Most likely: Mr. Associate Chief of Mental Health, MS. Nurse Manager for Primary Care; Dr. Chief of Pharmacy; Dr. Associate Chief of Pharmacy; Police Chief; Ms. Patient Advocate Manager; Chief of Prosthetics, Chief of Engineering, Chief of Supply Management; Ms. Nurse Manager Outpatient Clinic; Mr. Education; and about 75 leaders from all the departments; I was sitting up in front of the auditorium so it is difficult to list all who were present.

4. What did Mr. Director say to the angry patients at this time?

Nothing. He let them talk until they were finished. The patient speaking about Compensation and Pension acknowledged that he should stop and looked to Mr. Director to see if he could continue and Mr. Director gave him a nod to continue. I cannot recall if Mr. Director spoke or not. The patient did continue. I was concerned about how Ms. AO felt at the time.

5. How did the angry patients calm down?

They spoke for about 30–45 minutes each and eventually started to repeat themselves and knew it was time to stop. They vented directly at Ms. AO and me.

6. What did you expect Mr. Director to do while you were being ridiculed, harassed and personally humiliated by angry patients?

I expected Mr. Director to remind the patients to be respectful and not use names or titles. I expected Mr. Director to interrupt the patients when they singled out leaders in the audience. When the patients looked to him about time limitations, Mr. Director should have taken the opportunity to thank the patient and move onto the next guest.

We were told the patients wanted to let us know how we were doing as a facility, the good and the bad, so we can improve our customer service. This was not a town hall setting. This was Leadership Development Day, a learning environment.

7. After the angry patients left, did you tell Mr. Director that you felt harassed and humiliated by the angry patients? What was Mr. Director's response?

Mr. HR Chief spoke to Mr. Director immediately after the meeting and told him the meeting was inappropriate. Mr. HR Chief informed me of this encounter. The Leadership Development Day was on Tuesday, winter 2017. On the following day, I confronted the executive leaders at morning report and told them that I felt harassed at the Leadership Development Day meeting on Tuesday. I told them I was humiliated and that I expected Mr. Director to have intervened to stop the harassment. Mr. Director's Administrative Officer said the patients were told not to single people out by name or title. I then asked why Mr. Director did not intervene when this occurred. Mr. Director then stated, "I always believe the patients." Beyond this statement, I do not recall what else was said by Mr. Director. I do recall that I said that I did not want to be disrespectful in bringing this up at this time; but I wanted everyone to be aware that I felt embarrassed personally and professionally. I felt harassed. I referred to the core value of respect and requested that leaders along with patients be respected. I ended the conversation stating, "I expect Ms. AO felt the same way (embarrassed personally, professionally and harassed)."

I met with my supervisor individually to provide greater detail about my response to the meeting. My supervisor stated that the executive leadership team met with Mr. Director about the inappropriateness of the meeting and asked Mr. Director to apologize at the next meeting (a month later). The Chief of Staff, my supervisor said, "Mr. Director is unyielding." I asked for an apology. The next Leadership Development Day came and went. The chief of staff was not present. Mr. Director did not apologize. I met with Dr. Chief of Staff, my supervisor, upon his return and informed him that no apology occurred at Leadership Development Day. Ms. Mental Health Chief requested an apology also during a chiefs' meeting with Dr. Chief of Staff. I reminded Dr. Chief of Staff of this also. Dr. Chief of Staff said he would meet with Mr. Director. Mr. Director failed to apologize to the leadership group.

I recall the following as being present at morning report: Mr. Director; Ms. AO to the director; Dr. Chief of Staff; Mr. AO2 to Primary Care; Mr. AO1 primary care (He was not at the Leadership Development Day meeting however), others I do not recall.

8. Why did Mr. Director make the comment, "I always believe the angry patients"?

Mr. Director says this regularly to me.

Background: When Mr. Director first arrived at the end of 2016, he asked the leaders what he could do to support us and we went around the table. When my turn came, I asked him to please support opioid safety and the primary care providers. I asked for a meeting with Mr. Director and Dr. Chief of Staff. Ms. AO to the Director set this up. I ended up speaking to Mr. Director and Dr. Chief of Staff after a morning report. I had a report to show Mr. Director of my findings regarding opioid safety diversion, doctor shopping, patient overdoses, patient arrests due to selling their opioids. He did not want to see the report stating, "I will always believe the patients." I explained that we have an opioid epidemic in the United States and not only at the large health care system. Patients and community members are overdosing every day and some of our patients are not truthful in what they are doing with their opioid medication so we need to be firm with applying opioid safety initiatives. He stated, "I will always believe the patients." That was the end of the meeting.

Dr. CoS asked to speak with me alone and said all Mr. Director heard was me saying patients are diverting and he was angry. Dr. CoS said he was not happy that I requested the meeting and I should have discussed this with him. I replied that I always discuss this concern with him and that the new director needed to be informed and educated in order to support the primary care providers. I reminded him that patients will usually complain to the patient advocates, chief of staff office, director's office, and politicians. Those who were making money most likely feel desperate and will complain to try to get their opioids back to sell. I said I understand their desperation, but we as doctors cannot be suppliers.

Mr. AO1 to Primary Care began presenting weekly for us at morning report. He related how patients on opioids affected our access (the only thing the executive leadership team wanted to hear about and this was plainly stated by Dr. CoS). At the end of each PowerPoint report, Mr. AO1 had a slide asking the leaders to support the primary care providers (These reports are available if needed.) Mr. Director regularly reminded us at those morning reports that he would "always believe the patients [when they complained]."

On one of my last days prior to retirement, I was part of a rapid performance improvement team to address opioid safety. Very few leaders attended the meeting. I chose not to be part of the presentation to avoid expected harassment and our group agreed. The topic of diversion, doctor shopping, etc. came up along with how the patients complain. The Rapid Performance Improvement Workgroup (RPIW) group asked for Mr. Director's support. Mr. Director started speaking and presented his ideas which appeared to be upsetting to the RPIW group and uncomfortable to the small audience. I reminded Mr. Director at one point where this topic was brought up that he repeatedly states, "I will always believe the patients." He replied with a softer version; but I am well aware of what he repeatedly stated to me and primary care service leader regularly.

Those in attendance at the RPIW report out: Mrs. Systems Redesign and RPIW leader; Mrs. Quality Management; Dr. CoS; Mrs. PCP, NP, Mr. AO1 Primary Care; others

Audience: Dr. Chief of Pharmacy; Dr. Associate Chief of Pharmacy; Dr. Chief of Informatics; others

9. Did you tell Mr. Director that he had created a hostile work environment by not saying anything to the angry patients when they were ridiculing and humiliating you and what was his response?

Yes, I answered this above.

10. Why did you feel your sex (female) and age contributed to this incident with Mr. Director?

I have not witnessed Mr. Director belittling any of the male leaders publicly. He allowed the patient meeting to occur on leadership day and failed to take charge of situation which grew out of control. Ms. AO to the DCOS, female, about my age or possibly older was also a victim of harassment that day. Mr. Director embarrassed me and harassed me regularly at morning report. Mr. Director publicly embarrassed and harassed me in the spring of 2017 during a meeting he called for leaders in the auditorium.

Mr. Director has developed the reputation of having his good ol' boys with him and these are young men. One gave my photograph to be released to news without my permission; Mr. Access, Mr. AO to the Associate Director.

11. Did you report Mr. Director to the next higher-level official that you were being harassed because of your sex and age? If yes, to whom, on what date and what was the response? What action was taken if any after reporting the incident?

Mr. Director is our highest official at this facility. I reported his actions to my supervisor, Dr. CoS.

I reported Mr. Director to oversight committees of the large health-care system such as this office and I have spoken with multiple ERO officers and the Hassle Free Office. During the spring of 2017, I contacted Mrs. Hassle Free from the Hassle Free Office and she directed me to the Equal Rights Organization (ERO) Office because I had lost promotional opportunities due to Mr. Director's actions (more than what I described above). She stated this is an Equal Rights Organization (ERO) discrimination case since employment promotional opportunity was something I lost and is a condition of employment. I was to contact the ERO office within 45 days.

Prior to speaking with Ms. Hassle Free, I met with Mr. Facility ERO, the facility's ERO expert, to gather information about reporting an ERO concern. This is documented at the facility's ERO office.

During the spring of 2017, I contacted ERO, ORM 1-888-555-FAIR. What led me to ultimately report Mr. Director was the second leadership meeting humiliation event directed towards me and encouragement by another female leader who stated after the meeting, "You have grounds for filing an ERO complaint; Mr. Director would never do that to a man." A second leader stated something similar. I had an immediate visit by a third leader to see if

I was alright. I wasn't. That afternoon, my privileges were suspended and ordered by Mr. Director. The Professional Standards Board, Clinical Executive Board were not involved which is a violation of the facility's medical bylaws and Large Health-care System policy.

12. If you did not report this incident, explain why not. Not applicable

13. How were you harmed in this incident?

I was personally and professional humiliated in front of a group of 75-100 of my peers. As opioid safety initiative facility champion, I lost the ability as a leader to apply opioid safety initiatives at the primary care level for our facility. A non-medical, nonclinical leader, Mr. Director, made it clear he and other leaders did not respect me as a mature female leader. Essentially, I could not carry out my medical, ethical, legal, professional duties as ACOS for primary care and opioid safety champion when my privileges were suspended. Not only was I affected, the other female leaders were also affected, fearing the same treatment by Mr. Director and told me this fact.

14. Can you suggest witnesses who can provide relevant information? If yes, identify by name, title, and nature of information to be provided?

Witnesses are listed above with titles. Leadership day attendance records are kept by the director's secretary. We had a sign in attendance sheet.

15. Is there anything you would like to add? Yes, if more information is needed and requested.

Claim #2. From Winter 2016, to Spring 2017, Mr. Director humiliated complainant during the Morning Report and Leadership meetings.

1. How often do you have morning report and leadership meetings?

    Primary Care presents weekly during Morning Report. Leadership development days are monthly.

2. On what date in the Winter of 2016 did you meet and how did Mr. Director humiliate you during this meeting?

    On Leadership Development Day and is described above. The next day at Morning Report Day I discussed my concerns. Weekly, primary care presents about access and included request for opioid safety since this fell on primary care and is intimately tied to our national access movement goals.

3. Who was present during this meeting?

    Morning Reports: Mr. Director; Dr. Chief of Staff; Mr. AO1 for Primary Care, Mr. AO2 for Primary Care; Ms. AO to Director; Dr. Pain Psychologist, my Co-champion for Access; Mr. Access, leader for access; Nurse Executive; Mr. Associate Director (former Acting Director who was very supportive of leaders and opioid safety initiatives), and others intermittently

    Leadership development days: executive leadership team, Mr. HR Chief often presented topics along with others. Attendance sheets should be kept by the director's secretary.

4. On what dates did Mr. Director humiliate you after Winter 2016?

    The other leadership meeting where I as humiliated was Spring 2017. Weekly morning reports since Mr. Director's arrival at the end of 2016, escalating on and after Winter 2016.

5. Were the same people present during those meetings?

    During the spring of 2017, only one group of leaders were in attendance. Morning report described above.

6. What happened after the spring of 2017, that Mr. Director stopped allegedly humiliating you during this meeting?

    My privileges were summarily suspended twice by Mr. Director, in the early spring of 2017 and mid-spring of 2017 following reinstatement of my privileges and ACOS position three days prior to the second removal of privileges. By internal and external medical chart review, my privileges were fully reinstated without any findings on the internal and external reviews at the end of the spring in 2017.

    Shortly after my privileges were reinstated, I was served a proposal for reprimand citing not following policy regarding opioid safety, very similar to the reason for summarily suspending my privileges. I had seven days to respond to Dr. CoS. I had to meet face-to-face with Dr. CoS in the fall of 2017. I had an interview out west scheduled at that time and I had to change my plans. Dr. CoS then went on leave and failed to attend the meeting. I was not allowed to change the date for my face-to-face meeting with Dr. CoS, even though he would not be in attendance. I was to meet with Dr. New DCOS, the new deputy chief of staff, and he did not even know about the meeting that day or the circumstances. He appeared very surprised at the proposed reprimand. Dr. New DCOS contacted me at home while I was injured asking me to return to my associate chief of staff (ACOS) for primary care position because I was so good at my job. The reprimand was not approved in the end; but because I was interviewing for a new job, I had to disclose this possibility because I had to wait for the decision.

    Also, prior to this time, I lost my position as medical director, East Coast Hospital, a promotion which I accepted during the site visit during the spring of 2017. I put an offer on a house by the shore during the trip and it was accepted. My privileges were suspended three days later and I was to start my new job very soon. The East Coast Hospital could not wait for the resolution of my privileges, so they went with their second choice.

I interviewed for two other promotional opportunities for chief of staff at another neighboring facility and primary care service line director at still another facility in another northeastern state. References were checked and I received promising feedback and glowing reviews. I believe that in the end, the political press that followed me ("google" my name) made these facilities nervous and I was not hired. I did disclose the situation I was in initially and why I was leaving my present position. I was asked to provide references immediately after the interview and I received good feedback.

I had two significant physical injuries requiring extensive rehabilitation in the spring and summer of 2017 so I was out for rehabilitation and Family Medical Leave Act (FMLA) for extreme situational anxiety and insomnia resulting from the harassment preventing my return to the facility under the leadership of Mr. Director and Dr. CoS at this point. It became obvious that these two executive leaders, politely stated, were not supportive and looking for ways to terminate me after more than 15 years of service.

7.   During or after the meetings, did you tell Mr. Director that you were humiliated by his actions? If so, what was his response?

I reported harassment to my supervisor, Dr. CoS on or about the spring of 2017. I met with Dr. CoS for 90 minutes to review the reasons I could no longer stay at the Facility by the River. I informed Dr. CoS that I was considering filing an ERO complaint regarding continuous harassment by Mr. Director. This was an exit interview and notice of my plan to leave the facility. Dr. CoS stated he was saddened by this and commented that he had a tear in his eye. I spoke with Dr. CoS, my supervisor, on that spring meeting in 2017 about the harassment endured at the leadership meeting on that morning. Dr. CoS was not in attendance and stated he would speak with Mr. Director. I shared with Dr. CoS that another female leader encouraged me to file an ERO complaint of harassment by Mr. Director during that meeting.

Dr. CoS made it very clear that I was not to meet with Mr. Director following the initial meeting I requested with Mr. Director and Dr. CoS. I was told I was to go to him (Dr. CoS) and not include Mr. Director. See above for more detail.

8. Did you tell Mr. Director that you felt his behavior created a hostile work environment and if so, what was his response?

Only once as described above. My supervisor, Dr. CoS stated I was not to meet with Mr. Director. I was to report concerns to him as my supervisor.

9. Did you tell Mr. Director that you felt he was harassing you because of your sex? If yes, what was his response?

No. I reported being harassed for my sex to Dr. CoS.

10. Did you tell Mr. Director that you felt he was harassing you because of your age? If yes, what was his response?

No. I do not recall if I remember reporting harassment because of my age to my supervisor, Dr. CoS.

11. Did you report Mr. Director to the next higher-level official that you were being harassed because of your sex and age? If yes, to whom, on what date and what was the response? What action was taken if any after reporting the incident?

I reported this to ERO and other oversight bodies. There is action being taken by ERO and other governing bodies. Most action is in the investigation stage presently.

12. If you did not report this incident, explain why not. Not applicable.

13. Why did you feel your sex and age contributed to you being humiliated you during the morning report and leadership meetings?

    Ms. AO to the DCOS and I are both older female leaders and we were singled out during the leadership meeting. Mr. Director turned to me at many morning reports and said, "I will always believe the patients." He did not address his statement to Mr. AO2 or Mr. AO1, even when Mr. AO1 (young man) presented. I have not witnessed Mr. Director acting inappropriately to men in general and young men in particular.

    Mr. Director has been investigated for similar allegations while he was a military leader. This was published in the local newspaper. I do not know the outcome or full story other than what is stated in the newspaper article ("google" Military Director).

14. Did the harassment cease after you reported it to the agency? Explain.

    No, I actually had to retire early because I could not tolerate the harassment. I applied for other leadership and primary care positions beyond our facility. I believe that I was no longer a desirable candidate because of the television news story which is a false report supported by Mr. Director and Dr. CoS. If my name is "googled," this story pops up. I interviewed for chief of staff at a neighboring facility and my references were all checked, and the references were glowing. I believe the news story and other political events resulted in me not being selected. All of these negative events were initiated or supported by Mr. Director and Dr. CoS. I believe Dr. CoS fears Mr. Director and complies with Mr. Director's direction, fearing loss of his job and position.

15. Do you know if Mr. Director has harassed any other employees? If yes, who and how do you know they were harassed?

Ms. AO to Deputy Chief of staff and compensation and pension leader as stated above.

Dr. Pain Psychologist also confided in me about harassment from Mr. Director during meetings with him. I do not know the details. She is female and I am not sure of her age other than she is younger than me.

Mrs. PCP, NP was unfairly terminated from employment at the facility's clinic. I agreed that she should be reprimanded or suspended for her actions; but she was a strong provider who had not had any previous reprimands. She was merely trying to survive basically being the only provider handling a full schedule, all walk-ins, and all provider telephone calls and alerts for the busy clinic during a time of extreme provider shortage overall for the facility.

The Administrative Board (AB) recommended some type of reprimand or suspension. The politician recommended termination in the television news story, newspaper articles, and letter to the director of the large healthcare system.

I met with Dr. CoS and Mr. Chief of HR about Mr. Director's decision to terminate Mrs. PCP, NP. Mr. Director followed our appeal process; but I was told by Dr. CoS that Mr. Director intended to terminate Mrs. PCP, NP. Dr. CoS did not agree with the termination (but followed Mr. Director's direction), stating this was her first offense. I expressed Mrs. PCP, NP provided outstanding care and yes, made a big mistake, but not one rising to the level of termination. Mrs. PCP, NP is female and about my age.

Dr. PCP1 has been a target of the director because patients complain about her. She is a strong opioid safety provider. According to Dr. PCP, Dr. CoS and Dr. New DCOS have been harassing her and she is leaving the large health-care system because of the harassment. She filed an ERO complaint too I believe based upon sex and age. She is female and about my age.

Mr. Director and Dr. CoS looked into firing Dr. PCP2, clinic primary care provider and would not approve my request of sending another provider to the clinic to assist until after the Ignorant Oversight Body (IOB) report came out, even though I requested assistance in writing months prior. Dr. PCP2 was harassed for not being efficient when she was trying to follow the executive leadership team's face-to-face visit requirements for opioid safety and reported she could not get seventy-five patients into her schedule that month to Dr. CoS and me. Dr. CoS stated, "Don't let Ms. Nurse Executive hear this, but it is impossible to see everyone face-to-face." He went on to say that sometimes you have to do have telephone visits or let the nursing staff help you (to Dr. PCP2). This upset Dr. PCP2 because she wanted to see them all face-to-face reporting the patients on opioids had been mishandled previously overall. Dr. PCP2 asked for additional help. I requested assistance from Dr. CoS but the available provider would need to stay overnight during the week days. I explained this is common practice to Dr. CoS. He declined the request. Following the investigative report and news story in the spring of 2017, Dr. COS approved lodging and Dr. PCP3 helps out regularly. This all came about too late for Dr. PCP2. She quit recently because of lack of support and harassment. She is female and younger than me.

Dr. PCP1 and another female doctor (who would like to remain confidential at this time) feel harassed working under the leadership of Mr. Director and Dr. CoS. They are female and just a little younger than me. They are concerned about our facility's leadership.

16. Can you suggest witnesses who can provide relevant information? If yes, identify by name, title, and nature of information to be provided.

Dr. Psychologist; she witnessed the Spring 2017 meeting and expressed her concerns as to how I was treated based upon my sex.

Dr. ACOS for acute medicine was present for the Winter 2016 and spring 2017 meetings. She is also part of the Professional Standards Board and Clinical Executive Board. She expressed concern as to how I was treated for the previous events described above.

Chaplain was present for the leadership meetings. He is a direct witness of my condition following the humiliating meetings.

Another leader approached me about the spring meeting and her concerns.

Mr. Chief of Human Resources was present during the winter meeting and met with Mr. Director immediately following the meeting to address the inappropriateness of the meeting content. He is intimately involved with all of the summary suspension and reprimand proposal.

Ms. Mental Health Chief and Mr. Extended Care and Rehab Chief were at the February leadership meeting. Ms. Mental Health Chief requested an apology from Mr. Director at a Chief meeting with Dr. COS shortly after the event. They both are on the Professional Standards Board (PSB) and Clinical Executive Board (CEB) and participated during the month my privileges were suspended.

Mr. AO1 for Primary Care understands opioid safety concerns and a non-clinician. He is intimately involved with opioid safety complaints coming from the patient advocates, chief of staff's office, director's office, and political inquiries. He was present at the morning report meetings.

Dr. Chief of Pharmacy and Dr. Associate Chief of Pharmacy were present during leadership day meetings and were present during the RPIW opioid safety report out.

Dr. Chief of Informatics was present at the RPIW opioid safety initiative report out and probably present during leadership day meetings. She and her staff worked closely with me regarding opioid safety. Ms. Informatics1 and Ms. Informatic2 are two of her employees I interacted with regularly.

Ms. Patient Advocate Manager and I did not always agree on opioid safety initiative (OSI) actions, but she expressed concern that Dr. CoS would not acknowledge being aware of our opioid safety initiative actions. Dr. CoS was intimately involved and supportive until the spring of 2017.

Mr. Former Nurse Manager of Acute Psychiatry (he may have left the large health-care system) reached out to offer support following the leadership day in the winter of 2016. He stated he liked Mr. Director; but what he allowed to happen was wrong and he would support me if I needed support.

The employee survey will most likely contain statements regarding harassment, hostile leadership, retaliation. I understand the comments will go to the office of inspectors and the executive leadership team.

Mr. Police Chief was most likely present at leadership day. He is very knowledgeable about my efforts and opioid safety as part of our OSI workgroup. He can testify that Dr. CoS was very aware of our efforts and supported opioid safety efforts until the spring of 2017.

Ms. Quality1 and Ms. Quality2, RNs in quality management, are very knowledgeable about the behavior by Mr. Director and Dr. CoS towards me.

Mrs. Systems Redesign leader is very aware of the facility and opioid safety efforts. Support from the executive leadership team regarding opioid safety formally started after the investigative report and television news story were released in the spring of 2017...the good that comes out of the bad.

The opioid safety initiative workgroup members who attended our meetings can testify to our efforts, successes, and awareness by Dr. CoS. Mr. Secretary to COS would have some attendance records and agendas.

17. Is there anything you would like to add? Yes, but time is limited. I can provide more information if requested.

Claim #3. During the spring of 2017, Director suspended complainant's Health Care Privileges.

1. Briefly summarize your position duties and responsibilities?

Associate Chief of Staff for Primary Care and Opioid Safety Initiative Facility Co-Chair, Access facility Co-Chair

Primary care providers are responsible to apply opioid safety initiatives to their medical practice for chronic pain patients on opioids. As the ACOS for PC and OSI facility prescribing champion, I became the "go to" person for OSI concerns, education, opinion for treatment, recommendations by not only primary care providers, but also pharmacists, mental health providers, emergency department providers, hospitalists, social workers, nursing staff and even the chief of staff. Previously, the acting director would consult with me regarding media and political inquiries centered around opioid safety. I provided guidance and responses on behalf of our facility for action plans centered around opioid safety for the internal inspectors, DEA, IOB, AO-IOB and others. The quality management department, director's office, chief of staff office and others would request my input regarding opioid safety efforts.

I supervise about thirty-five primary care providers and administrative staff and all that goes with quality reviews for medical records, credentialing and privileging, and more.

I am on too many to count committees at the facility and regional level, performance improvement projects. (If needed, I can provide a list.)

2. What are the Health Care Privileges needed to assist you in your position?

    Appointment to the medical staff by the Professional Standards Board and Clinical Executive Board, unrestricted state medical licensure

3. How did you learn during the spring 2017, that your Health Care Privileges were suspended and from whom?

    Dr. CoS came to my office and presented me the letter about the suspension. He stated Mr. Director ordered him to do this and he agreed to present me the letter.

4. What was Mr. Director reasons for suspending your health care privileges?

    This occurred two days after the television news story aired. The story went up to large health-care system headquarters and the headquarters pain specialist was told to investigate the situation. I was out on leave and unaware at the time. I was not included on any responses to large health-care system headquarters.

    I since learned that the investigative body released a report in the spring of 2017 which was very flawed. I have testified to this fact recently to the investigative board just prior to my unplanned early retirement in the fall of 2017. The politician saw the investigative report and wrote a letter to the president of the large health-care system with demands. Instead of supporting our opioid safety initiative efforts, Mr. Director and Dr. CoS chose to use me as the facility's "scapegoat" to appease the politician. Mr. Director's and Dr. CoS's actions are now under investigation with this ERO investigation and other investigating bodies. Dr. CoS stated to me that the investigative report was flawed and he intended to call the investigative board members to inform them. This was on during the spring of 2017.

I did not see the investigative report until it was included in my reprimand proposal in the fall of 2017. Dr. CoS's testimony to the follow up investigative office from the spring of 2017 was included in the reprimand binder delivered to my home under certified /receipt mail in the fall of 2017 just after my privileges were reinstated. The chief of staff's testimony is filled with untruths (lies) regarding a history of disciplining me for opioid safety, reason for Ms. PCP1 no longer being a large health-care system employee, and performance by Dr. PCP2.

I actually received an outstanding proficiency in the winter of 2016 citing leadership ability and OSI efforts/accomplishments and fully satisfactory (highest rating) on my midterm proficiency just two weeks prior to the summary suspension of my privileges in the spring of 2017. I was not disciplined; I was praised. The second investigative duo asked for proof. Dr. CoS could not provide this evidence because he had no evidence. The disciplinary incident presented by Dr. CoS was fictitious.

Dr. CoS was fully aware, actively participated, and fully supported our OSI efforts. He received praise by regional leaders about our improvement. Mr. Director received praise too for all of our efforts. Reports with data submitted monthly by Mr. AO1 for Primary care and regional opioid safety initiative reports submitted by the regional supervising office were presented to Mr. Director and the executive leadership team regularly by our primary care service line leaders during weekly morning reports.

5. What was your response?

I was shocked. I told Dr. CoS that he knows this is wrong. I informed Dr. CoS that I would need to take formal action. He said I have the right but asked me to wait a week. He wanted to speak with Mr. Director on Tuesday (Monday was a holiday) first.

I reminded Dr. CoS that I was fully informed by him and aware that Mr. Director had no intention of listening to Mrs. PCP1, NP as part of required appeal process for termination. Mr. Director merely went through the process to avoid questioning. The AOs for Primary Care were told to hire Dr. New PCP (vice PCP1, NP) for the clinic two weeks prior to Mrs. PCP1, NP's appeal. I expressed I was not in agreement as to how the director and he (Dr. COS) were handling these situations. I told him it is very unfair to employees to fail to follow processes. Dr. Cos tried to reassure me stating my "case was different" and that I "didn't do anything wrong" He stated I had a long career at the large health-care facility (ahead of me). I asked Dr. CoS how he could say that with what he was proposing, summary suspension. I asked if I could be given the opportunity to retire early on my birthday. He said I would not need to do that. I stated I did not do anything to deserve this... I was just implementing opioid safety. I said, "this is all political, just like Mrs. PCP1, NP's case."

I showed Dr. CoS the stack of emails I had been sending for the Accountability Office to the IOB since the day prior when I was interviewed and they requested. I stated if the second investigative duo is still investigating the original investigator's report and waiting for the requested evidence to support my testimony, how can this summary suspension be happening?

I reminded Dr. CoS of his full support for our opioid safety initiative efforts as service chief and OSI champion for the facility. I reminded him that we both know face-to-face visits with patients is best but absolutely not possible. He acted surprised by this statement and stated he "did not remember".

I then felt desperate and began to become emotional stating that I am the only support system for my family. I support my husband because he follows me around for my career, two step sons with extreme challenges, my mother and other family members on occasion. Dr. CoS stated he could get in trouble for telling me more and asked me to give him time…all would work out. I did not believe him even though I wanted to. Until now, he had been supportive, or so I thought.

I signed the letter proposing summary suspension of privileges.

6. Did you tell Mr. Director that you felt harassed in this incident? What so what was his response?

I told my supervisor, Dr. CoS. I did tell Mr. Director on the day our RPIW OSI group reported out just prior to my retirement that I was aware I was used unfairly as a scapegoat due to political pressures originating from Ms. Politician. Mr. Director ended up harassing me during the report out and I had the opportunity to share my side of the story. Mr. Director also harassed Ms. PCP, NP and Ms. Quality during their parts of the presentation (both females). Instead of listening to the report out which is the expectation, he "heckled" them with aggressive comments and abusive behavior. Mr. Director did not harass the male presenters.

7. Did you tell Mr. Director that you felt this incident created a hostile work environment based on your sex and if so, what was his response? If not, why not.

I informed Dr. CoS, my supervisor. I did not publicly state this during the RPIW OSI presentation. I try to remain respectful.

8. Did you tell Mr. Director that you felt this incident created a hostile work environment based on your age and if so, what was his response? If not, why not.

No. I do not recall if I reported age as a factor to my supervisor, Dr. CoS. I vividly recall stating sex as a factor.

9. Before your suspension, how long had you had your Health Care Privileges?

23 years without a blemish

10. Do you know of any other employees that had their Health Care Privileges suspended? If yes, please identify by name, position title, sex, age and explain why were they suspended.

I know of 2 doctors, Dr. 1 (male) and Dr. 2 (older female). I am not certain of the situation for these providers now; but I was mostly likely on the PSB/CEB at the time.

I was involved with and recommended Dr. PCP9 and Dr. PCP10's suspension of privileges with extensive documentation to support these recommendations.

Mrs. PCP1, NP was terminated despite that fact that the medical boards, Professional Standards Board (PSB) and Clinical Executive Board (CEB), recredentialed her and appointed her to the facility's medical staff just prior to her termination by Mr. Director.

11. Why do you feel that you were discriminated against based on your sex and age when your Health Care Privileges were suspended?

Please see above. As far as the summary suspension goes, political actions by Ms. Politician also influenced Mr. Director and Dr. CoS to take action. I do, however, believe they would not have done this to a man, especially if the man was a young man named Mr. Access, or Mr. AO to the Associate Director.

12. Did you tell your supervisor that you felt discriminated against based on your sex and age when your Health Care Privileges were suspended?

Yes, as described above.

13. Can you suggest witnesses who can provide relevant information? If yes, identify by name, title, and nature of information to be provided.

    Dr. ACOS Acute Medicine; Dr. Chief of Surgery; Ms. Chief of Mental Health; Mr. Chief of Extended Care and Rehab; others on the PSB/CEB. Mr. Credentialing would have the names as the leader for Credentialing and Privileging. Mr. Credentialing was present at the PSB meetings as was Mr. Credentialing's assistant at the time.

14. Is there anything you would like to add? Yes, if needed and requested.

Claim #4. As of the Spring of 2017, complainant's assignment as the Opioid Safety Initiative Co-champion ended as a result of the suspension of her clinical privileges.

1. How did you learn about your Opioid Safety Initiative Co Champion ending as a result of your suspension of her privileges and from whom?

   Without privileges, I could not practice medicine which serves as a basic criterion to serve as the facility's prescribing OSI co-champion. I was put on administrative, nonclinical duty by Dr. CoS.

2. How did your privilege effect your involvement with the opioid safety initiative co-champion?

   Please see above.

3. What was your response to this initiative ending?

   I contacted an oversight agency to report my concern that there would not be anyone to lead the facility in the opioid safety initiative (OSI) efforts. The primary care providers, mental health providers, pharmacists, nursing staff, ED providers, hospitalists would no longer have someone to consult and support their efforts. This could lead to an increase in unsafe practices because of known coercion by the Ms. Politician, Dr. CoS, and Mr. Director to reinstate opioids to known addicts, patients who are known to sell their medications, patients who are known to doctor shop in order to increase patient satisfaction for votes (Ms. Politician) or increase in patient satisfaction score ratings (Mr. Director) or fear of unemployment (Dr. CoS).

4. How did this incident effect your position?

I lost my position as medical director for East Coast Hospital because I did not have privileges on my start date in the late spring of 2017. I could not find employment at another facility within the large health-care system. I could not return to work at the facility due to the harassment, resulting in situational anxiety and insomnia. It was obvious to other staff at the facility that I was "a target". I feared losing my privileges, termination, and loss of my medical license. I retired early, taking over $1,000.00 monthly reduction in pension. If I could have returned or been hired at another facility, I would have been eligible for full retirement in four years or early retirement without reduction in pension in nine months based upon minimal age. I served the organization for just under 20 years.

5. What was management reasons and response to your concerns?

This is unknown as far as Mr. Director and Dr. CoS are concerned.

The primary care providers, administrative officers, ACOSs and chief colleagues, many pharmacists, many mental health providers, quality management colleagues, informatic colleagues, and others were saddened about what happened to me. I was told I deserved a medal for my OSI efforts, not to be used as a "scapegoat" by Mr. Director and Dr. CoS.

6. Do you know of any other employees that had their clinical Privileges suspended? If yes, please identify by name, position title, sex, age and explain why were they suspended.

Please see above.

7. Why do you feel that you were discriminated against based on your sex and age when your clinical privileges were suspended?

I am a strong female leader, with a wealth of large health-care system experience and training, who earned the respect of many colleagues as an advocate for primary care providers as the ACOS for primary care and opioid safety initiative prescribing champion for the facility I am told. Staff trusted me and reached out to me daily for assistance. I was always happy to help and serve as the buffer between the executive leadership team and the front line clinical staff as an advocate. (I do not believe the ELT appreciated this role; they would have preferred I take orders without question, especially after Mr. Director arrived.)

My goal was to take care of the employees who could then take care of the patients. This is why I pursued leadership training and a MBA in health care. When employees feel supported, they work harder to take care of the patients and they stay. We all know the number one reason people leave their jobs is due to an unsupportive boss. Primary care scored very high on the 2016 employee survey, boosting the facility's scores, resulting in our facility being one of the most improved in the nation last year for which Mr. Director and Dr. CoS were praised.

I believe Mr. Director is not capable of sharing the "spotlight" with a strong mature popular (according to others) female leader. Other employees shared these thoughts with me and I now believe they may be right.

Dr. CoS is just a weak leader, intimidated by Mr. Director. I pray he learns to support his medical staff and tell the truth. Actually, I believe he should consider resignation for his actions. Perjury is no small matter either.

8. Did you tell management that you felt discriminated against based on your sex and age when your clinical privileges were suspended?

Yes, Dr. COS and my supervisor, especially based upon sex. I do not recall if I mentioned age specifically although I do believe age is also a factor.

9. Was the harassment witnessed by anyone? If yes, who?

Please see all of the names previously mentioned.

10. Did you tell management that you felt harassed by this incident? If yes, what was his response?

I reported concerns to Dr. New Deputy Chief of Staff about my concerns and that he would most likely serve as OSI facility prescribing champion by default as Acting ACOS for primary care since opioid prescribing falls onto the primary care providers. Dr. New DCOS did inherit this title and unfortunately, he is following direction from Mr. Director and Dr. CoS, coercing primary care providers to reinstate opioids, slow opioid tapers, etc. when complaints are received by disgruntled patients. Dr. PCP has now left the large health-care system due to harassment from Dr. New DCOS under Dr. CoS's and Mr. Director's direction. Patient satisfaction is clearly valued over prevention of unintentional opioid overdose by patients and community citizens.

11. Did you tell management that you felt he was harassing you because of your sex and age? If yes, what was his response?

I told Dr. New DCOS who was Acting Chief of Staff in Dr. CoS's absence during the fall of 2017 during the reprimand proposal. This was all documented by Mr. Chief of Human Resources who was also in attendance. My attorney was present by telephone. Dr. New DCOS appeared surprised and shocked regarding the actions of Mr. Director and Dr. CoS. He appeared unaware of the reprimand. As part of the PSB/CEB meetings, he supported others to vote unanimously to reinstate my privileges mid-spring of 2017. The proposed reprimand addressed the same content as the summary suspension.

12. Did you report your supervisor to the next higher-level official that you were being harassed because of your sex and age? If yes, to whom, on what date and what was the response?

    What action was taken if any after reporting the incident?

    Yes. This would have been Dr. New Deputy Chief of Staff and Dr. Chief of Staff mentioned above. I included this in reports to other oversight bodies in the name of patient and community safety.

13. If you did not report this incident, explain why not.

    Not applicable.

14. Why did you feel your sex and age contributed to your assignment as the Opioid Safety Initiative Co-champion ended as a result of the suspension of your clinical privileges?

    It all goes together, like dominoes.

15. How were you harmed in this issue?

    Patients were potentially clinically harmed. Citizens were potentially clinically harmed. The river state residents were potentially clinically harmed.

    I lost an important role to help serve employees and the community. I suffered humiliation when I walked around the hospital as a patient and physician who had her privileges summarily suspended, medical expertise and 15-year experience dealing with opioid safety questioned publicly on television and in newspapers.

I suffered with situational anxiety and insomnia in anticipation of having to return to face more losses as an employee at the facility under the leadership of Mr. Director and Dr. CoS. I even avoided appearing in public wondering if I would be recognized and my husband and I started sitting in the back row at church because I felt humiliated and embarrassed (and we used to sit up in the front).

16. Was your job affected in any way? Explain your answers.

I believe I have covered this topic.

17. Do you know if management has harassed any other employees? If yes, who and how do you know they were harassed?

Previously addressed, please see above.

18. Can you suggest witnesses who can provide relevant information? If yes, identify by name, title, and nature of information to be provided.

Please see above.

19. Is there anything you would like to add?

If needed and requested.

20. 20. What remedy do you seek in this matter?

Consideration of termination of Mr. Director and Dr. CoS from large health-care facility employment or request for resignation.

Report of this case to go to the oversight committee regarding the actions of Ms. Politician and her use of coercion to reinstate opioids to known unfortunate opioid addicted patients we were trying to help and other patients known to clinical medical staff to not be using opioids safely or appropriately.

I request a respectful interview by the television newscaster who aired the false story or another newscaster (preferred) to tell my story and I will agree to be respectful.

I request a respectful apology to the employees of the facility and me by the facility's executive leadership team.

I request appropriate action addressing the release of my photograph to the television news station. This photograph came from a previous facility function and the photograph was only to be used for promotion of that function. Mr. Director is responsible for releasing the photograph. I did not sign for release of the photograph or give permission in any way for its use beyond access promotion the prior year.

Having been advised of the above information about my role as a witness in the investigative process, I solemnly swear _____ affirm _____ the statement which follows is true and complete to the best of my knowledge and belief, and addresses the issues and concerns raised with me by the investigator.

CHAPTER 10

Reprimand Proposal: The Discovery of the Inaccurate Ignorant Oversight Body Report and Its Effect

A false witness shall not be unpunished, and
he that speaketh lies shall perish

—Proverbs 19:9, KJV

I didn't know about the Ignorant Oversight Body report until the receipt of the reprimand proposal. The report was included in a binder prepared by the facility's human resource department.

Due to recent injuries and medical conditions, I spent time at home recuperating. The doorbell rang, which was unusual, and I greeted the mail carrier. I signed for a package from our facility. I opened the package and discovered a white binder filled with documents.

The binder contained the reprimand proposal; Dr. CoS's testimony to the Accountability Office to the Ignorant Oversight Body in response to the Ignorant Oversight Body report from the spring of 2017; my testimony to the Accountability Office to the Ignorant Oversight Body (AO-IOB); Memorandum from Dr. Prior COS dated in the winter of 2013; Facility Policy No. xxx, Pain Management, summer of 2015; Management of Patients on Long-term Opioid and Narcotic Medications, Policy No. xxx, Winter 2015; the IOB report from the spring of 2017; and the chart used by the IOB which was prepared by nonclinical clerical staff.

The Ignorant Oversight Body report unveiled conclusions by the IOB team which relied on a nonsensical graph and preposterous reports by angry nurses. The IOB team failed to interview providers. Other leaders were not interviewed. It perplexed me that such an official group from the head office could act upon such a limited and faulty investigation. Secondly, the investigative team failed to document their investigation with written testimony at that time. Not only did the team fail to report the truth, others acted upon their report. The politician wrote a scathing letter to the headquarters president with demands to take punitive action. Mr. Director and Dr. CoS acted upon the politician's recommendations recognizing the inaccuracies of the investigative report. The local newspaper published erroneous reports. Every action taken by these leaders were based upon one wrong erroneous report from the Ignorant Oversight Body which sadly has physician representation. Shame on them!

Every retributive action taken by these leaders landed onto my shoulders. They labeled me as the bad guy. They branded me as a terrible doctor. They pigeonholed me as their scapegoat! And for what reason? I believe it was all for political advancement in a corrupt system. I turned out to be dispensable. I, a strong mature female leader who stood up for what is true, what is important, and what is essential in preventing unintentional opioid overdoses in a country actively engaging in fighting an opioid epidemic, became the facility's victim. The executive leader did not value saving lives. He only cared about his selfish career pursuits. The politician did not value saving lives. She only cared about winning votes. The chief of staff did not value saving lives. He only valued retaining his position.

The investigative team returned to the facility for a second visit and asked questions about Dr. CoS. I interviewed with them and informed them of their faulty document as professionally as I could. They documented the second visit.

In response to the proposed reprimand, I addressed each of the enclosed documents. The first was the memorandum from former chief of staff, two years prior to my arrival dated during the winter of 2013 which addressed the clinical staff about interim guidance related to prescribing opioids for chronic pain.

This was my reply to this memorandum in response to the proposed reprimand:

- Dr. Sky was not a member of the facility medical staff until the fall of 2015
- Dr. CoS told Dr. Sky during the spring of 2017 that he was aware that she was not at the facility until two years later and she would not be expected to be aware of this memorandum.
- Dr. CoS was originally appointed as deputy chief of staff, acting ACOS for Primary Care during the timeframe shortly after the memo was issued during the winter of 2013 until Dr. Sky arrived in the fall of 2015 to assume the associate chief of staff for primary care position.
  - o Dr. Prior ACOS Primary Care was made a fulltime provider due to a provider shortage prior to Dr. Sky's arrival.
  - o Dr. Clinical Manager1 was detailed to full time provider due to provider shortages prior to Dr. Sky's arrival.
  - o Dr. Clinical Manager2 was detailed to full time provider due to provider shortages and behavioral concerns prior to Dr. Sky's arrival.
  - o Providers left primary care due to high demands for opioids, lack of leadership support, and double booking prior to Dr. Sky's arrival. (See Evidence 1-Power Point with turnover)
- Face-to-face visits were required every 4 months for stable patients who took opioids for chronic pain and every 2 months for unstable patients; however, the details of the

state medical law regarding opioid was unclear and questions were still being asked in 2017. (Enclosure)

- o Compliance with face-to-face visits were not being monitored by the facility's prior COS or prior DCOS who was Acting ACOS for PC (currently the COS).
- Prescription monitoring reports were to be run at the beginning of the opioid treatment plan and at least annually after. This was to start in the winter of 2014. Dr. Prior COS and Dr. CoS (at that time titled DCOS and acting ACOS for PC) did not comply with this requirement. Dr. Sky arrived in the fall of 2015.
  - o Very low compliance with this action request from the winter of 2013 memorandum was noted for the number of patients on opioids for chronic pain during 2015 (See Evidence)
  - o Compliance increased when Dr. Sky arrived with Dr. Sky being the highest user of the prescription monitoring program in assisting PC providers and as opioid safety initiative champion prescriber.
- A drug monitoring test must be performed at the beginning of treatment and at least annually after. To start during the winter of 2014.
  - o Urine Drug Tests were being performed prior to Dr. Sky's arrival but the staff did not know how to interpret the results and there was minimal action on inappropriately negative drug results or cannabinoid use. Dr. Prior COS and Dr. CoS (at that time titled DCOS and acting ACOS for PC) did not understand and/or educate the staff about urine drug screen (UDS) interpretation. The Pain Management Opioid Safety A Quick Reference Guide (2014) was available for use under the opioid safety initiative toolkit webpage since 2014 (Enclosure). Dr. Sky arrived in the fall of 2015 and educated the staff about UDS interpretation and the need to flag the UDS to receive the results when the UDS is inappropriately negative. Dr.

Sky educated the staff that a different order is needed for fentanyl, oxycodone, and tramadol. The staff was ordering UDS, fentanyl, oxycodone, and tramadol for many patients when this was not required and the laboratory costs were very high.

o   Dr. Sky educated the medical staff about urine drug test result interpretation and the need to alert oneself to receive results of the urine drug test in order to catch inappropriately negative results.

o   Dr. Sky educated the medical staff about the need to order fentanyl, tramadol, and oxycodone as a separate test. (See Evidence 3- Urine Test Interpretation and Evidence 4- Pain Management Opioid Safety A Quick Reference Guide (2014)-Dr. Sky printed colored copies of this reference for all of the Providers with instruction.

o   There is no mention of the need for a face-to-face visit when inappropriately negative drug screens are found or other similar behavior associated with diversion. There is no mention of who communicates treatment plans to the patients in this document.

•   In summary, the facility was not following this document to its fullest extent. Dr. Prior COS and Dr. CoS (at that time titled DCOS, acting ACOS for PC) were leaders during the time this document was released and the document was signed by Dr. Prior COS. If the information was to be enforced by the ACOS for PC, that would have been Dr. CoS's responsibility. Dr. Prior ACOS for PC had been detailed to work as a primary care provider. Later, Dr. Prior ACOS PC rarely came to work. The facility had one of the highest numbers of opioids distributed across the country prompting visits by the Drug Enforcement Agency (DEA) in winter of 2015 and another inspection team in the spring of 2016. Dr. Sky started in the fall of 2015 and was not part of the DEA visit. Dr. Sky assisted the facility in applying opioid safety initiatives when she arrived. She became a co-champion for the facility and was instrumental in improvements and education of the entire clinical staff along with Dr. Pain Psychologist. (Enclosure as OSI champions)

- Dr. CoS was the chair of the opioid safety workgroup. Dr. CoS failed to attend and lead many of the OSI meetings and Dr. Sky and Dr. Pain Psychologist ran the meetings. (same enclosure as above)
- Dr. Sky and Dr. Pain Psychologist educated the clinical staff at medical staff meetings, primary care town halls, mental health meetings, emergency department meetings, patient advocate meetings, and more.

This was my response to the pain management in the fall of 2015 facility policy addressing the proposed reprimand:

- A stepped care strategy and approach to managing patient's pain is to be implemented
  o Dr. Prior COS and Dr. CoS, (formerly DCOS, acting ACOS for PC) were leaders at the time of the development and initiation of the policy.
  o Primary care providers had no pain management education, urine drug screen interpretation education, or program expectation education. The providers received a copy of Dr. Prior COS memorandum (above).
  o Dr. Pain Psychologist, AO Acute Medicine, ACOS Acute Medicine, Surgery representatives were meeting to discuss a plan for pain management upon Dr. Sky's arrival. Dr. Sky became an active participant. Later, pain management was moved from acute medicine to surgery.
  o Dr. Sky, ACOS for primary care became the facility's OSI champion prescriber because the primary care providers were the only clinicians assisting with opioids. (same enclosure as above) Dr. Sky was filling in

for many missing providers initially from four facility locations:

- Team Red, Team White (2 providers), Team Blue (2 providers)
- Team Green, Team Orange (2 providers)
- Team Yellow, Team Purple (2 providers)
- Team Brown (1 provider)
- (Enclosure from PowerPoint also with missing staff)
- The facility has not progressed much past Step One in the Pain Management Clinic Model as of fall 2017.
- The facility attempted to develop STEP Two. There is a pain interventionalist, 2 physiatrists, and a pain psychologist assigned to the pain clinic.
  - o Dr. Sky discussed her accomplishments at the facility with the initial group meeting under acute medicine and later at executive leadership presentations
  - o Dr. Sky forwarded the pain management STEP TWO model to Mr. Director upon his arrival. Dr. Pain Interventionalist concurred. There has been no action to "beef up" our pain management efforts until the spring of 2017 due to political pressure.
  - o Presentations to executive leaders and politicians express having a pain management opioid prescriber on board within a month or two by Dr. CoS. Dr. CoS stated this to the opioid safety rapid performance improvement workgroup report out audience at the end of the summer of 2017. There has not been a pain management prescriber hired. There is another interventionalist hired that will not be prescribing opioids.
  - o The primary responsibility for opioid prescribing and OSI efforts still remains on primary care providers.
  - o Dr. CoS does not have a DEA license. He will not prescribe opioids but he will ask pharmacists to fill opioids under another provider's name and ask other providers to fill opioids against their assessment. He

contacts primary care providers to write for, initiate, reinstate and/or increase opioid doses in patients when the PCP is not in agreement. He will also contact the pharmacy to fill opioids under the name of the PCP. (See Evidence)

- A multidisciplinary pain medicine committee is to facilitate and implement this policy. The committee has not been very effective but does meet. This committee does not meet regularly and is not a known resource to most of the providers.

- The policy discusses offering alternatives for treatment. Dr. Sky has been very instrumental in leading the effort to supply pain prosthetics, eliminating barriers for ordering pain management devices (Enclosure), suggesting chiropractic care in the pain clinic and acupuncture. Dr. Sky has helped to remove barriers in this area, removing the need to get physiatry approval. Mindfulness and music therapy have been added since Dr. Sky's arrival. These non-opioid alternatives were not addressed by Prior COS or Dr. COS (former DCOS and acting ACOS for primary care) prior to Dr. Sky's arrival.

- Face-to-face visits are only addressed in this policy for the required four-month visit.

This was my response to Management of Patients on Long-term Opioid and Narcotic Medications Winter 2014 Policy and the proposed reprimand:

- Dr. Prior COS and Dr. CoS (former DCOS, acting ACOS for PC) were responsible for following this policy prior to Dr. Sky's arrival.
- Dr. CoS does not have a DEA number.
- Dr. CoS does not prescribe opioids.
- Dr. CoS does not see patients face-to-face when reviewing opioid requests and this occurs almost on a daily basis.

- Dr. CoS did not know how to review the electronic medical record thoroughly and frequently asked Dr. Sky to assist him.
- Dr. CoS frequently documented trusting Dr. Sky's judgment when reviewing opioid requests as a covering provider for multiple medical home teams simultaneously, facility wide (multiple sites) opioid safety initiative prescriber. (Enclosures)
- Dr. New DCOS initially was able to meet with patients face-to-face for opioid medication reviews. However, since Dr. New DCOS has been acting ACOS for primary care, Dr. New DCOS can no longer meet with patients face-to-face when recommending dose adjustments, etc.
- Dr. CoS (formerly DCOS and acting ACOS for PC) and Dr. Prior COS failed to follow policy. They were to report drug diversion or illicit drug use to the police according to policy.
- Dr. Sky reported drug diversion initially on two occasions. This reporting was not supported by the facility at the time. The chief of police did join the OSI workgroup and attended regularly. Police have been called due to unruly behavior by patients centered around opioids. The police were always ready to assist. (Enclosure)
- Dr. Sky and the opioid safety initiative rapid performance improvement workgroup team did discuss this present part of the policy on RPIW report at the end of the summer of 2017 with Mr. Director, Dr. CoS and the audience. Mr. Director said we can report suspected diversion to the group. Dr. Sky confirmed this on by email form with the executive leaders and RPIW team members. (Enclosure)
- Face-to-face visits are only mentioned in regard to every four month requirement by State Law PL 2013 for patients on opioids for chronic pain exceeding fifteen mg morphine equivalent and exceeding sixty opioid pills per month. This policy does discuss seeing patients face-to-face every two months if tapering, changing the dose, etc. (Enclosure)

The State Law PL 2013 is not included in the review but is referenced. This is my response to the law and reprimand proposal:

(e) If a test performed under subsection (a), or conducted under subsection (d), renewals inconsistent medication use patterns or the presence of illicit substances, a review of the current treatment plan shall be required. Documentation of the revised treatment plan and discussion with the patient must be recorded in the patient's chart.

- The law does not state who needs to do the discussion with the patient (Enclosure)
- Medical Home PAIN Roadmap discusses the team approach as do other Medical Home documents
- Ms. Nurse Executive did not want the nurses to tell the patients because the patients acted poorly. Nurse Executive insisted the providers have face-to-face discussions with the patients according to discussions I had with Dr. CoS. Dr. CoS shared this with Dr. PCP also.
- Dr. CoS told Dr. Sky that nursing was insisting. Dr. Sky agreed this would be best, but physically impossible to do so as a rule. Dr. Sky was pain champion for the facility and fielding opioid safety calls, questions, electronic medical record notes from many different locations on a daily basis. It was impossible for Dr. Sky to call every patient she reviewed and this is not an expectation for facility champions.
- Consults are placed every day to specialists. Every consult is reviewed by a chart review and often, a chart consult is all that is required. Electronic consults are standard practice at the large health-care and in the community. Workload credit is given. Electronic consults often involve medications with side effect possibilities, etc.
- Face-to-face visits for inappropriately negative urine drug screens are not needed. If there is no opioid in the urine, the patient is not ingesting the opioid for chronic pain. He/she most likely does not have pain. Why would a face-to-

face be needed to address a treatment plan for pain? This would take away access for true conditions.

- Patients do not always tell the truth and/or do the right thing. Why do certain leaders believe the patient and not check the other side of the story, the clinical side?
- There is much documentation that diversion, doctor shopping, illegal activity, etc. exists. One city has the highest overdose rate. Is it possible that our patients could be selling their medications to make a living? (See Enclosure-Arrested Patient)
- If a patient is visiting fifteen to eighteen different medical practices and filling opioids at each location in many different cities, at many different pharmacies, is a face-to-face visit required? Minimally, this puts the office staff at risk, especially in the outpatient clinics without police presence. Following our policy and reporting such activity to the police is prudent to investigate. A phone call to the patient is much safer for staff.
- Dr. Prior COS and Dr. CoS (former DCOS, and acting ACOS) did not advise providers to see patients face-to-face for all opioid safety contact prior to Dr. Sky's arrival. In fact, the primary care providers had very little support to initiate opioid safety initiatives prior to Dr. Sky's arrival as reflected by the extremely high numbers of opioid tabs being prescribed, especially from two specific cities.
- Face-to-face visits were only discussed after December 2016 as being preferred. This was *never* referenced as being part of law or policy other than the four-month rule/two months for adjustments. If this were not true, Dr. CoS (former DCOS, acting ACOS) and Dr. Prior COS failed to follow policy/law every time they reviewed an opioid request and told the provider to change their plan without seeing the patient.

This was my response to the Ignorant Oversight Body's spring of 2017 report in relation to the proposed reprimand:

- The Chart sent to the IOB group was inaccurate
    - "Not applicable" should have been an option; if Dr. Sky did not change the prescription, why would there be a discussion with the patient since she was the covering provider? Why would other staff need to discuss anything with the patient since there are no changes? Why would consults be placed if Dr. Sky was merely asked to do a refill? Why would there be discussion of a taper when Dr. Sky did not change the prescription why would the clinical pharmacy specialist be needed? (Enclosure)
    - The preparers of the report were non-clinical, a clerk and an administrative officer without clinical experience. They defaulted to mark "N" (no) when the question did not make sense making the report nonsensical, inaccurate and invalid.
    - The patients who needed tapers were informed by nurses in all cases which is standard practice with requests for any medication refill or communication with the patient (See Enclosure Medical Home). The investigators stated that the nurses were *not* informed by Dr. Sky. Dr. Sky cosigned nursing staff in all of the cases where communication was needed.
    - Dr. Sky arranged for face-to-face visits by covering providers. (See same Enclosure as previous 41 pages) This is standard practice for primary care ACOSs who are short staffed. The ACOS would not be expected to go to each clinic located in different cities across the state to see patients to do refills. This requirement would be geographically impossible to accomplish. To complicate the situation further, the previous administration did not implement opioid safety initiatives and the number of opioids being prescribed were

extremely high. The numbers of opioids dispensed by this facility was one of the highest if not the highest *of all the facilities in the system nation wide.* This attracted attention from the DEA, IOB, Oversight Committee, and politicians.

o   Dr. Prior COS and Dr. CoS (formerly DCOS, Acting ACOS for Primary Care) were responsible for opioid safety initiative implementation and oversight and they failed to address these safety measures as part of their professional responsibilities.

o   Dr. Sky arrived at the facility in the fall of 2015 and immediately began to address and implement opioid safety initiatives. It was under Dr. Sky's leadership that the facility began to improve on OSI measures, educate staff across the facility, and prevent unintentional overdoses both for patients and the community.

o   Dr. CoS supported Dr. Sky's efforts and leadership for the opioid safety initiative until the spring of 2017 when the Ignorant Oversight Body report was released. (See Enclosures)

- All of the patients that were reviewed from the clinic had telephone contact by their Medical Home team nurses when opioid safety initiative education was needed (See Enclosure). Dr. Sky routinely cosigned the Medical Home team nursing staff to assist with the care of their team's patients. This occurred on all of the patients reviewed. The investigative report on page xxx states "Dr. Sky did not always inform patients or the clinical team of her plans to taper…" *This is a completely false statement and can be verified in the clinical record.*

- Dr. Sky then offered face-to-face appointments for patients with covering providers: Dr. PCP1, NP1; Dr. PCP2, NP2; Dr. PCP3, NP3; Dr. PCP4. The clinical pharmacy specialist and providers were consulted and worked with patients who needed tapers. The investigative report states that "Patients were tapered off of their opioid pain medications without close clinical supervision…" *this is a completely false statement and can be verified in the clinical record* (See Enclosure Summary pages). It was not the standard of care nor should it be standard of care for a covering provider, opioid safety initiative champion, consultant, associate chief of staff, chief of staff to see every patient face-to-face while providing coverage across the state for refills and other needs which do not require face-to-face visits. A covering provider should *not* be expected to follow *unsafe inappropriate* prescribing practices of colleagues in their absence. It is much more important to *prevent unintentional overdoses immediately* when the covering physician *uncovers unsafe inappropriate* prescribing practices. Often, this is done by giving the patient a partial supply, checking pill counts when high numbers of pills are prescribed, checking electrocardiograms (EKGs) for methadone patients, checking urine drug screen results, checking the state Prescription Monitoring Program, checking frequency of pill fills and quantities.

- Dr. Prior COS and Dr. CoS (former DCOS, acting ACOS PC) did not monitor prescribing habits of the primary care providers except when a patient advocate, congressional, regional, or other inquiry brought concerns to their attention. At that time, by primary care provider report, the primary care provider would be contacted by the leadership team member to make the patient happy resulting in coercion to ignore opioid safety practices. Primary care providers feared implementation of opioid safety initiatives prior to Dr. Sky's arrival.

- To repeat, Dr. Sky could not be at many locations every day. The numbers of opioid refill requests outnumbered the hours in the day due to previous opioid dispensing practices and loss of providers. Dr. Sky did hire three fee basis providers to help fill in the gaps and provided gap coverage across the facility. Dr. Sky was the only provider willing to help with opioid refill requests. If Dr. Sky had refused to refill the medication without a face-to-face visit, as discussed with her by Dr. New DCOS, patients would not have received any opioids across the board. Dr. CoS does not fill opioid medications at all. Can you imagine the complaints?

- Face-to-face appointments are not required for *all* opioid changes with examples to follow. If this is implemented, *access will be immediately affected negatively.*
- "Tapering" was used inappropriately to have many meanings. Tapering is defined as reducing opioid doses increments to try to prevent withdrawal symptoms.
- Patients cannot die from tapers, even fast tapers. They can feel sick; but they cannot die.
- "Tapering" has been misused to also mean "not renewing" when there is no drug in the urine. No drug in the urine means the patient is not ingesting the medication and tapering would not be needed. Medications for any withdrawal symptoms were routinely offered to all of the patients by Dr. Sky. Face-to-face visits are not needed when the patient is not ingesting opioids for pain.
- "Tapering" has been misused to also mean "not renewing" when the patient is filling opioids in the community. Dr. Sky did not "taper" if the patient was seeing a dentist or had an acute needed. Dr. Sky "did not renew" the opioid when the patient was filling opioids from fifteen different providers at six different pharmacies while filling opioid monthly at the facility. Face-to-face visits are not needed to inform the patient that he or she violated the pain agreement.
- The patients suspected of diverting or using illicit substances should have been reported to the police department according to current policy. Dr. Prior COS and Dr. CoS (former DCOS, acting ACOS for primary care) failed to follow policy.
- Dr. Sky tried to follow policy to report suspected diversion to the police; but this was not supported at the time by the executive leadership team, many whom were "*acting*" and

unfamiliar with the policy and /or were worried about the political implications.

- Dr. CoS confessed to Dr. Sky in the spring of 2017 that the Ignorant Oversight Body report was very flawed. Dr. Sky requested a copy of the report; but she did not receive it until the summer of 2017. Dr. CoS stated to Dr. Sky that he planned to call the IOB investigators to report his concerns. Dr. CoS stated he had discussed his intentions with another executive leader.

- Dr. Sky did not violate state law or medical center policy in regard to face-to-face appointments. This requirement was made up by the executive leadership team in response to nursing complaints. Dr. Sky acknowledges how difficult implementing opioid safety initiatives has been for the facility, especially during a time where primary care providers were at an all-time low. However, the medical home team, does require action by team members. Dr. Sky did provide coverage for face-to-face visits for the patients by other primary care providers. Again, Dr. Sky exercised standard practice for addressing refills during provider absence and this is common practice across the facility, especially in rural areas.

- Dr. Sky has the greatest amount of experience with opioid safety initiative implementation as a primary care provider, previous pain clinic supervisor (fifteen years). Dr. CoS hired Dr. Sky due to her leadership and pain management experience. Opioid prescribing falls onto primary care providers at the facility and Dr. Sky, associate chief of staff and opioid safety initiative facility prescribing champion assisted clinical staff across the facility.

- Dr. CoS relied on Dr. Sky to assist him in his clinical reviews for opioid safety. Dr. Sky and Dr. CoS communicated regularly about opioid safety initiative challenges and successes. The primary care administrative team presented data, challenges, recommendations, and other educational information to the executive leadership team and clinical staff regularly. Dr. CoS appeared to have been supportive until late spring of 2017.

- The Ignorant Oversight Body recommends "appropriate, educational, administrative, or disciplinary accountability to the ACOS, PC." The Professional Standard Board and Clinical Executive Board recommended an award be given to Dr. Sky for her efforts for opioid safety initiative implementation.

- All of the clinic patient charts were clinically reviewed internally and externally twice. The clinical oversight boards determined no fault in the clinical practice by Dr. Sky for the clinic patients and the patient who died from severe coronary artery disease. The clinical oversight boards ruled in favor of Dr. Sky's clinical practice finding no fault in the manner in which Dr. Sky followed medical staff policy and State Law. If fault were to be found in following medical staff policy, then Dr. Prior COS and Dr. CoS would need to be reviewed and reprimanded. These men were leaders during the implementation of the state law, memorandum, and policies.

- Dr. CoS had reviewed the state law and informed Dr. Sky and the Professional Standards Board in the summer of 2017 that there was no clear direction that the face-to-face visit requirement served as any value for medication adjustments other than fulfilling the state required 4month/2month visits. The law states that communication regarding treatment plans must be given to the patient; but the law does not specify *who* must communicate with the patient. Medical Home Handbook and Medical Home Pain Roadmap clearly encourage teamwork and communication to patients by the team. Dr. Sky provided coverage for face-to-face visits by fee basis PC providers, staff PC providers, and clinical pharmacy specialist providers. These providers were able to assess the patients and discuss recommendations with the patients in a timely manner. The covering providers were able to use their clinical judgement. At no time had Dr. Sky coerced a provider to prescribe against their medical judgement. Dr. Sky was careful to use words such as "recommend," "consider." Dr. Sky frequently reviewed this with the primary care providers during provider meetings. Dr. Sky earned the respect of her providers. Dr. PCP4 texted Dr. Sky to show support in the fall of 2017. Other providers have reached out to Dr. Sky to show support and appreciation for her efforts. (Enclosure)

- Dr. Sky agrees with the Ignorant Oversight Body that sufficient qualified provider staffing at the clinic take place. Dr. Sky had hired a full staff of primary care providers across the campus. Unfortunately, with the recent actions taken by the director and chief of staff involving Dr. Sky and double booking on over-paneled teams, this may continue to be a challenge.

"A false witness shall not be unpunished, and he that speaketh lies shall not escape"
—Proverbs 19:5, KJV

This was my response to Dr. CoS's testimony under oath to the Accountability Office to the Ignorant Oversight Body in the late spring of 2017. Can you say perjury?

- Dr. Sky includes this review of Dr. CoS's testimony as evidence to question the integrity of Dr. CoS and his leadership capabilities. Dr. CoS does not speak the truth during his testimony and he is under oath.
- On page xx, line xx, Dr. CoS describes verbal counseling to Dr. Sky in the fall but he cannot find any paperwork on the discussion. This is because this interaction did not occur.
- Dr. Sky received an outstanding proficiency in the winter of 2016 citing her efforts in opioid safety initiative implementation and other aspects of her leadership in primary care. (Enclosure)

- Dr. Sky received a "Fully Successful or better" which is the highest mark on her midterm proficiency dated late spring 2017. (Same Enclosure)
- Dr. Sky received outstanding proficiency ratings throughout her career.
- Dr. Sky was officially recognized as the facility's co-champion along with Dr. Pain Psychologist (previous enclosure)
- Dr. Sky was consulted by facility leaders to assist with Drug Enforcement Agency (DEA), Ignorant Oversight Body (IOB) and other oversight bodies related to opioid safety. (Enclosures)
- Dr. CoS conferred with Dr. Sky regularly as an opioid safety initiative resource. Mr. Acting Director and the facility's associate director regularly consulted Dr. Sky about opioid safety information.
- Mr. Director contacted Dr. Sky and the primary care staff regularly for opioid safety initiative updates and data to be presented to community partners.
- Dr. CoS states on page xx, lines xx that he did not know the extent of the clinic coverage for Dr. Absent PCP. Dr. Sky informed Dr. CoS immediately and regularly of findings at the clinic and Dr. Absent PCP's patients. Dr. Sky put Dr. Absent PCP on a focused professional performance evaluation (FPPE) for cause because of the extent of her discoveries. Dr. Sky tried to explain the situation at the clinic and share her Prescription Monitoring Program findings with Mr. Director upon his arrival in Dr. CoS's presence. Mr. Director did not want to review the material and Dr. CoS expressed displeasure with Dr. Sky for asking to speak with Mr. Director about the situation. Dr. Sky explained the seriousness of her findings at the clinic and the need to be sure the new director was aware.
- Dr. CoS declared he could not find documentation of the verbal counseling with Dr. Sky on pages xx and xx. Dr. Sky received praises, not counseling. Dr. CoS relied on Dr. Sky's experience and knowledge base. (Enclosures- emails from Dr. CoS).

- Dr. CoS states that PCP, NP left the clinic leaving an unexpected absence of a provider. PCP, NP was terminated and this was planned by Dr. CoS and Mr. Director in advance. Dr. Sky expressed disagreement with this plan on numerous occasions with Dr. CoS and Mr. Human Resource Chief. The request to human resources is included. (Enclosure)

- Dr. CoS states Dr. PCP will not ask for help from nursing. Actually, Ms. Primary Care Nurse Leader called Dr. Sky twice to say Dr. PCP asks for too much help from nursing. Nursing and medical home team assistance is an expectation as part of the medical home model and Medical Home Pain Roadmap (Enclosure).

- Dr. PCP saw all of her opioid patients face-to-face before refilling because almost all of the doses need to be reduced and/or safety items needed to be reviewed. Dr. PCP, Dr. Sky, and Dr. CoS talked on a conference call. Dr. PCP reported that she could not feasibly get all of the patients in before doing opioid renewals. She needed 75 slots additional appointment slots. Due to the high number of patients on opioids for chronic pain at the clinic, it was impossible to see all of the patients face-to-face.

- Dr. CoS stated Dr. PCP4 was sent to the clinic due to staffing shortages at the clinic. This was not the reason Dr. PCP4 was sent to the clinic. Sending Dr. PCP4 to the clinic resulted in many reports of contact by staff and patients due to her behavior which was well known to many employees and patients at the facility.

"The LORD preserveth all them that love him:
but all the wicked will he destroy"
—Psalm 145:20, KJV

I learned what most likely happened. Just search my name and all of the lies pop up. I now have to endure social media humiliation the rest of my life. Thank you, Dr. CoS! Thank you, Mr. Director!

Thank you, Ms. Politician! Thank you, Ms. Television Newscaster! Sleep well.

> "The fear of the LORD prolongeth days: but the
> years of the wicked shall be shortened"
> —Proverbs 10:27, KJV

This was our rebuttal to the reprimand proposal and included supporting documents. Dr. CoS did not show for the face-to-face meeting. Dr. New DCOS, very unaware of the situation, was called at the last minute to attend. Mr. HR Chief was present and took notes of the meeting which I have not seen or reviewed for accuracy.

> "He giveth power to the faint; and to them that
> have no might he increaseth strength"
> —Isaiah 40:29, KJV

Date: Fall 2017
From: Dr. B. Sky, Associate Chief of Staff, FBTR Health Care
           System
Subject: Response to Notice of Proposed Reprimand Letter Dated
           Summer 2017 *Proposed Reprimand Received Summer 2017,*
           Response Due
           Summer 2017

To: Dr. Chief of Staff, FBTR Health Care System

Dear Dr. Chief of Staff,

The large health-care system has proposed reprimanding me for "Failure to Follow Medical Center Policy" because I allegedly "reduced the level of opioid prescriptions for multiple patients without properly assessing these patients, as required by local Medical Center policy."

These charges are false and the reprimand proposed against me should be rejected because they are based on an obvious misinterpretation of the policy the Medical Center had in place, the practices I followed had previously been implemented by the Medical Center Chief of Staff, and those practices were in keeping with both sound medical practice and the standards endorsed by the State Medical Board.

First, as noted by the Ignorant Oversight Body report, the Medical Center has adopted the State Medical Board's opioid safety guidelines as its official opioid safety policy. In Fall 2014 the Medical Licensing Board of State established requirements for the prescribing of opioid controlled substances for pain management (available at **http://www.stategov/legislative/iac/20141105-IR-844140289FRA.xml.pdf**). Those standards were issued in response to growing concerns about over-prescription of opioids and were meant to curb the dangers trend of opioid addiction. The relevant section of the rule reads in its entirety as follows:

Sec. 6. (a) ***Physicians shall not prescribe opioids for patients without periodic scheduled visits.*** Visits for patients with a stable medication regimen and treatment plan shall occur face-to-face at least once every four (4) months. More frequent visits may be appropriate for patients working with the physician to achieve optimal management. For patients requiring changes to the medication and treatment plan, if changes are prescribed by the physician, the visits required by this subsection shall be scheduled at least once every two (2) months until the medication and treatment has been stabilized. (emphasis added)

Reading the entire paragraph of the standard, it is clear that the Medical Board's intent is to bar physicians from issuing further opioid prescriptions without periodic scheduled visits. The Medical Center, however, has chosen to misread this paragraph in a way that flies in the face of common sense.

The Medical Center is claiming in this proposed reprimand that the final sentence of the paragraph should be read in isolation as a command that all patients must be seen every two months if any changes are to be made to their opioid prescriptions, including tapering or suspending their prescription. ***In other words, the Medical Center is claiming that physicians must continue prescribing opi-***

oids to patients at current levels if patients do not attend continuing evaluations.

Reading the rule that way would mean than once a patient is prescribed opioids that patient has the sole power to continue their prescription in perpetuity if they simply avoid showing up to any more doctors' appointments. Clearly, that is not in keeping with sound medical practice or the State Medical Board's intent to reduce opioid dependence.

Rather, the correct understanding of the rule the Medical Center is now falsely claiming I violated is that *physicians should only prescribe opioids to patients if those patients attend evaluations at least every four months (or two months for patients undergoing changes to their prescription regime) and if the patient chooses not to attend those evaluations those prescriptions should be tapered or suspended.*

If there is any doubt that this is the correct interpretation of the rule, the State Medical Association's summary of the rule, updated Fall 2016, should put that doubt to rest (available at **http://www. ismanet.org/PDF/LEGAL/statePAINMANAGEMENTPRE-SCRIBINGFINALRULESUMMARY.PDF**). That summary clearly states "*No prescribing [opioids] without periodic scheduled visits*" and that "any time the physician determines that it is medically necessary, whether at the outset of the treatment plan, or any time thereafter, a prescribing physician shall perform or order a drug monitoring test."

Second, the procedures I followed were in keeping with the Medical Center's existing policy as articulated by the State Medical Board and by Dr. CoS; as well as previously implemented by Dr. Chief of Staff in his capacity as the previous Opioid Safety Co-Chair. The FBTR Health Care System's existing policy has been to evaluate the etiology of patients' chronic pain, develop a treatment plan to address the pain with a focus on function offer alternative treatments for chronic pain including Physiatry and Pain Specialty consultation, Complementary Alternative Modalities; and non-opioid pain medications. Pain agreements, Urine Drug Screens, limiting number of opioids dispensed to a thirty-day supply, discouragement of early refills, limiting number of opioids dispensed from the Urgent Care or Emergency Room, use of a risk report are addressed in current policy. Use of the Pharmacy Medication Prescription Report, face-to-face visits, and tapering guidelines are not in the current policy. Diversion and illicit drug use is addressed in the current policy. The Associate Chief of Staff, Primary Care Services and Nurse Managers, Ambulatory Care have oversight of Management of Patient on long-term Opioid and Narcotic Medication. The Chief of Staff over-sees the Pain Management Policy. The specific examples below and attached show this to have clearly been the case:

- The Pain Management Policy outlines a step care strategy to address pain. I outlined a step care plan suggestion to Mr. Director, Dr. Chief of Staff, Dr. Surgery, and Ms. AO to the Directory on Winter 2016. Dr. Pain Interventionalist supported my suggestion which was in line with policy. To date, the policy and directive have not been implemented (Enclosure 5). Dr. Chief of Staff is responsible for this policy.
- Staff education is mentioned in the Pain Management Policy. The staff received minimal education about the Opioid Safety Initiative prior my arrival in the fall of 2015. Dr. Pain Psychologist and I educated the medical staff about opioid safety (refer to Medical Staff agendas). I educated the staff about interpretation of urine drug screen and other OSI topics using the Opioid Safety Initiative Toolkit (Enclosure 3) http:// PAINMANAGEMENT/Opioid Safety Initiative Toolkit.asp and Pain Management Opioid Safety A Quick Reference Guide (2014). (See medical home agendas and medical home steering agenda)
- I sent clarification to the Primary Care Providers and others about interpretation of the State Pain Management Prescribing Final Rule Winter 2106. There was confusion about interpreting the final rule as late as this year. The investigative bodies assessed FBTRHCS practices from the spring to the fall of 2016. The Chief of Staff and other clinicians continued to have questions about State Law regarding opioids to this date. (Enclosure)

- I participated on a Rapid Process Improvement Workgroup in the summer of 2017. This workgroup addressed the interpretation of State Law pertaining to opioids and the group was told to keep "within the spirit of the law," reported by Dr. Pain Psychologist as coming from Mr. Director. The "spirit of the law" concern was addressed at a RPIW follow up meeting in the fall of 2017 by the group with Mr. Director and clarified with the Director that the group should follow the law, period. Witnesses for the fall meeting: Mrs. Systems Redesign, Dr. Pain Psychologist. (Enclosure RPIW slide)
- Dr. Chief of Staff thanked me in the summer of 2016 for my "continued leadership in assisting us (FBTRHCS) in carefully reducing the use of opioid among our patients. We know this is challenging, but it is vital that we continue to pursue this." (Enclosure)
- In the spring of 2017 Dr. Chief of Staff stated before the Medical Center's Professional Standards Board that he had reviewed the State Medical Board's standard and concurred that Medical Center physicians are not required to meet with patients face-to-face before issuing a taper or suspension of opioids.
- Finally, you preceded me in overseeing opioid safety standards at the Medical Center. During that time, you oversaw the same policy you are now accusing me of violating such as reviewing electronic medical record charts and making clinical recommendations about opioid use without face-to-face visits (i.e.: provider reviews, political inquiries, internal inspector hotline inquiries, regional inquiries). You and the providers under your leadership did not use the state Prescription Monitoring Program regularly. You and your providers under your leadership did not know how to interpret urine drug screens. You and your providers under your leadership did not do pill counts for safety checks. You and your providers under your leadership had not identified complementary alternative medicines prac-

tices or refer patients for alternative care. You did not report illicit drug findings and diversion to the police. You did not initiate a step plan for pain management. Your previous practice shows both that I did not violate Medical Center policy and that the Medical Center's attempt to discipline me now is arbitrary and motivated by retaliatory motives.

As the above examples show the medical center had no policy against reducing patients' opioid prescription levels without an in person visit and there is no basis for saying I violated any such policy.

Finally, the practices I followed at the Medical Center were in keeping with generally accepted sound management of opioids. I addressed inappropriate urine drug screen findings, I updated state prescription monitoring reports on almost if not every chart I reviewed for the primary care staff, pharmacists, social workers, patient advocates, political reviews, and others. I assisted FBTRHCS and supported appropriate OSI actions. I am including a sample of my findings over a six-month period of time. (Enclosure)

When covering for providers on leave and when assisting others, I encouraged UDS updates, pill counts, pain agreement updates, face-to-face visits with covering providers, state Prescription Monitoring Program use, reduction of opioid doses, caution with using opioids with benzodiazepines, caution with using opioids if patients had chronic medical conditions in which opioids for chronic pain are contraindicated (i.e. obstructive sleep apnea, COPD). All of these actions are encouraged as part of the CDC, OSI toolkits, and ongoing developing policies, handbooks, and directives.

As you know, I fought long and hard to implement an opioid safety policy at the Medical Center in keeping with the current medical standards. Claiming that I should be reprimanded for trying to save patients' lives by following those guidelines is the height of irony and shows the illegal retaliatory motives of the large health-care system in acting against me.

In sum, the large health-care system is not proposing that I be reprimanded for breaking Medical Center policy, it is cynically proposing that I be reprimanded for following widely accepted and medically necessary opioid safety standards. There was never a policy at the Medical Center against tapering or suspending medications for patients who did not show up for appointments, the medical standards I established and followed at the Medical Center were sound, and those practices were in keeping with both the letter and spirit of the very regulation the Medical Center is accusing me of violating.

Therefore, it is clear that this proposed reprimand should be rejected.

In the end, I did not receive a reprimand. However, unfairly, I received a written counseling. Although insignificant pertaining to requirements of professional disclosure, the counseling based on lies was unjustified and unwarranted. I will live with this outcome. This action made it clear I could not return to the facility. Lord only knows what Mr. Director and Dr. CoS would pull next to humiliate me or worse yet, jeopardize my medical license. I had to retire. I had no other choice.

"Be of good courage, and he shall strengthen
your heart, all ye that hope in the LORD"
                                                        –Psalm 31:29

CHAPTER 11

Complaint Department Office

For which cause we faint not; but though our outward
man perish, yet the inward man is renewed day by day.
For our light affliction, which is but for a moment, worketh
for us a far more exceeding and eternal weight of glory.

—2 Corinthians 4:16, 17 (KJV)

I researched oversight committees and learned about the Complaint Department Office. This committee "handles claims of wrong-doing within the large organization from current employees, former employees, and applicants for employment." The disclosure unit takes reports regarding "violation of a law, rule, or regulation." I sent the following letter to the Complaint Department Office:

I am a board-certified family practice physician, and a military general medical officer, four years in private solo practice and fifteen years at the large health-care system. I have fifteen years of experience addressing opioid safety initiatives at the large health-care facility, first as a primary care provider for eight years, primary specialty service line director developing a multidisciplinary pain management group for a facility for five years, and associate chief of staff for primary care charged with initiating opiate safety initiatives (OSI) as the facility OSI champion along with a pain psychologist for two years. I was recruited by this facility because of my leadership, pain management clinic development, and opiate safety initiative experiences.

OSI efforts all fall onto primary care at this facility. I am an advocate for primary care providers across the facility as the associate chief of staff for primary care, opioid safety initiative (OSI) champion position for the facility, and OSI representative for the regional committee for pain management. Our efforts in primary care in applying opiates safety initiatives efforts were highly supported by the chief of staff and service line leaders including but not limited to pharmacy, mental health, acute medicine, prosthetics, extended care and rehabilitation chiefs. The newly appointed chief of staff, previously deputy chief of staff, had minimal to no knowledge of pain management and opioid safety initiatives until I arrived. As previously stated, this is one of the reasons I was recruited to this facility.

One city which our rural clinic served was an outlier in number of opiates dispensed. The Drug Enforcement Agency (DEA) investigated our facility in the winter of 2015. The internal inspectors investigated our facility in the spring of 2016. This same city also has one of the greatest populations of unintentional overdoses in the country. Prior to my arrival in the fall of 2015, there was minimal application of OSI requirements except for completion of pain agreements. Primary care providers did not have much leadership support because the primary care leaders were assigned to care for patients due to a large exit of primary care providers from the facility. Since my arrival, the facility has been educated on interpretation of urine drug screens, pharmacy database access and use, use of pill counts, use of clinical pharmacy specialists to assist a tapering, OSI education and more. All of the patients taking opiates received a letter to explain opioid safety initiatives to prevent unintentional overdoses in June 2016. Political partners received a letter to explain OSI intentions in the early summer of 2016. Our providers, nursing staff, and administrative staff for primary care spent hours on the telephone speaking with patients about opiate safety. Face-to-face discussions are encouraged at every visit. Unfortunately, some patients remain unsatisfied. We are working to continue to improve our services both at this facility and through networking in the community. We now provide prosthetic devices to help with pain, chiropractic care, acupuncture, aqua therapy, physical therapy, physiatry, and other non-narcotic medications for pain and more. All of our efforts have been reported back to the investigating officials.

As opioid safety co-champion along with the pain psychologist and associate chief of staff for primary care, I assist with chart reviews as requested by the chief of staff, primary care providers, pharmacists, other medical providers, nurses, administrative staff, and others often offering recommendations to consider or help with interpretation of test results, etc. If a provider is on leave, I will often assist with renewals of opiates since we do not have a pain management department prescriber, although this is in the works. With my fifteen years of experience in this field, I can offer suggestions in many if not most cases. I partner with the clinical pharmacy specialist for tapers. Some patients do not need tapers if there is no opiate in the urine on the drug screen and the opiate is simply not renewed. Mental health providers are co-located in primary care and we have a warm handoff policy to assist any patient in need. Our efforts have greatly increased over the past eighteen months since my arrival.

I earned the respect of many my colleagues in leadership, pharmacists, primary care providers, specialty providers, nurses, and clerical staff. My goal has been to advocate for clinical staff with the thought that if they feel supported, they will take good care of the patients. Primary care scored very high on our employee survey and the results were exciting.

The director started at the large health-care system at the end of fiscal year 2016. Our primary care service leaders presented OSI history, goals, and accomplishments on numerous occasions to the director and executive leadership staff. Our primary care service explained the primary care turnover concerns in the past, our challenges, and our recent successes (almost fully staffed in all locations once our recent hires start soon). Access for care is our goal; same-day access and we are almost there. To retain primary care providers, I stopped overbooking upon my arrival and negotiated for administrative time weekly. Overbooking and lack of administrative time leads to provider and clinical staff burnout and turnover. Recently, the director made the decision to restart overbooks for primary care providers and this was implemented while I was away on leave in the late spring of 2017. Additionally, the chief of staff participated on a television news interview were my name was used repeatedly, my photograph was shown without my permission violating Policy (1), and my professional and personal reputation was disparaged. I learned about the news story airing while driving home back from leave at the end of early spring 2017. I participated in OSI educational programs on the radio in the past and I was the person contacted by the news station initially. I later learned that this was not to be a friendly interview. I declined the interview; but the chief of staff participated. The chief of staff had been supportive of our opioid safety-initiated efforts for the entire eighteen months I had been at this facility. I had a midterm evaluation late spring 2017 and was rated as fully successful. I was rated as outstanding on my fiscal year 2016 proficiency citing opiates safety initiative accomplishments as a major factor. Our efforts in primary care, although difficult to measure, have helped in the prevention of unintentional overdoses for patients and the community. We still have much work to do in hour efforts.

On a Wednesday in the late spring, the city paper published a very unflattering article. The politician is quoted vilifying our facility and the large health-care system in general based upon one-sided deceptive reports by untruthful patients. Many politicians contact our facility on behalf of patients. This is standard practice. Primary care leadership reaches out to the patients on behalf of the facility regarding opioid safety concerns. We are knowledgeable team. We provide the written responses to the official inquiries. One politician however, has been relentless. She continuously "over advocates for patients" not understanding their clinical history and she ultimately coerces the executive leadership team of the facility, most notably the director (no clinical knowledge) and chief of staff to act upon inaccurate clinical reports. The chief of staff in turn oftentimes asks me for chart review and recommendation; but with continued pressure by the politician and the director, both without clinical knowledge, the chief of staff has been reported to approach primary care providers without my knowledge to "reconsider opioid plans." Often, I am notified by these providers and/or pharmacists who fill the prescriptions that they are feeling coerced into doing something unsafe for the patients which could result in unintentional overdose and death. Specific examples can be shared.

In the late spring, a news story aired and featured patients stating they were "cut off" without communication and the politician ridiculed opioid safety efforts by the large health-care system. The story also featured the chief of staff for a facility, who made ill-informed comments about facility provider practices which I found surprising since he had been supportive of our OSI efforts all along. Additionally, the chief of staff had been positively recognized, along with the director, for our OSI best practices at the facility. The documentation to prove why opiates were stopped for safety reasons is easily located in the medical records. The politician, newscaster, and chief of staff failed to check facts prior to airing the story. These facts, of course, may not be shared publicly due to HIPAA rules which was one of the reasons I declined the interview.

The news story exploited my name extensively in a derogatory manner during the broadcasting of the story. As previously mentioned, my photograph was released without my permission by the director, violating Policy (1) and the photograph appeared throughout the report. As opioid safety provider champion for the facility and associate chief of staff for primary care with fifteen years of primary care, pain management, and opiate safety experience at the large health-care system, I would be the physician staff consulted to for advice. Chart review is a standard practice for champions and associate chief of staffs to use and involved reviewing the state prescription monitoring program site, medication list, opioid agreement, urine drug screen, pill counts, radiographs, provider note history, and other appropriate information. When the urine does not have the drug in the urine and the patient is filling that opiates in the community and at the facility regularly, the opioid agreement (reviewed and signed by the patient previously) has been violated. It is standard practice not to renew opiates at the facility or in the community if the opioid agreement is violated. Patients are informed the findings by a primary team member in a respectful manner. Additional care is offered.

At the end of late spring 2017, I returned to work from leave. The following day, I received a summary suspension of privileges citing aspects of my practice "do not meet the excepted standard of practice and constitute an imminent threat to patient welfare." I understand the director ordered the chief of staff to recommended immediate summary suspension of privileges in response to public embarrassment and political pressure, abusing his authority has director. The chief of staff agreed and issued a summary suspension of privileges, abusing his authority has chief of staff. Issuing a summary of privileges is warranted only when "sufficient evidence exists, based on the preliminary fact-finding, that a practitioner may have demonstrated substandard care, professional misconduct or patient care." The director and chief of staff failed to follow procedures and processes clearly outlined in the medical staff bylaws and policy regarding credentialing and privileging. Actions by the director and chief of staff were carried out in haste and retaliatory nature in response to public embarrassment and political pressure.

Primary care providers at the facility presently do not have a supportive leader or opioid safety initiative champion provider to consult regarding opioid safety concerns. Several of the strong ethical providers, unwilling to be coerced by the director and the chief of staff, are now being targeted for removal from employment. An ethical provider at a contract site was recently given an employment opportunity at the facility. I understood that the employment offer was going to be rescinded and indeed it was rescinded, again reflecting the political environment and abuse authority by leaders previously mentioned. The physician is a highly respected leader in the community.

Many of the service line leaders and chiefs reported concerns that their privileges and employment may be terminated at the whim and abuse of the authority of the director and chief of staff succumbing to public embarrassment and political pressure.

Lastly, there is a substantial danger to public health and safety if the facility and the community fail to initiate and uphold opioid safety measures. Leaders, political representatives, and others have the right to inquire about their patients' and citizens' concerns. These concerns are routinely investigated and communicated to the patient and office submitting the inquiry as part of our daily work in the primary care administrative office. The leaders, political representatives, and others do not have the right to abuse their positions of authority and coerce physicians to prescribe or treat patients when the providers know their recommendations may result in iatrogenic harm to patients including unintentional overdose and death related to opioid prescribing. Nonclinical leaders, political representatives, and others do not know the clinical background of the patients and citizens they serve. Clinicians know the clinical history of the patients and citizens they serve. Leaders, political representatives, and others do not have the right to abuse their positions of authority to suspend a provider's privileges, rescind employment offers, or threatened termination of an employee based upon misleading reports.

The city that had the highest rate of unintentional overdose rates in the state is also one of the highest across the country. We owe it to our patients and community citizens to prevent unintentional overdoses and risk of death related to opiates. The Centers for Disease Control (CDC) guideline for prescribing opiates for chronic pain is our major source for OSI guidance and goals as a nation. A large health-care system leader put out a memorandum on December 2014 with the subject titled: Opiates Safety Initiative Updates with goals and guidance. The large health-care system has an opioid safety toolkit (http:// PAINMANAGEMENT/Opioid_Safety_Initiative_Toolkit.asp) to use for guidance with a multitude of resources. These professional clinical references and others have been asked extensively over the past 18 months at the facility under the primary care and OSI champion leadership in collaboration with other service line leaders, clinical pharmacy specialists, pain psychology champions, and others and full support by the chief of staff until recently.

To mention, I am a wartime Veteran who served as a general medical officer for the military stateside. My son is an Iraqi wartime combat Veteran suffering from wartime disabilities. He would have been homeless without my husband's and my support. He receives care presently at the large health-care system.

I heard from an attorney from the Complaint Department Office. She requested examples of coercion in redacted documents. I sent her email communication from physicians reporting contact from Dr. Chief of Staff requesting reinstatement of opioids for known addicts and other patients who had been taken off of their opioids for chronic pain due to illegal activity or other medical indications. I spoke with the CDO attorney in the early summer of 2017. I didn't hear back until the fall 2017 due to unfortunate circumstances in her life. The case was active in this oversight office until the winter of 2017.

> "Though I walk in the midst of trouble, thou wilt revive me: thou shalt stretch forth thine hand against the wrath of mine enemies, and thy right hand shall save me"
> —Psalm 138:7, KJV

CHAPTER 12

Time to Retain a New Attorney

Let nothing be done through strife or vainglory; but in lowliness
of mind let each esteem other better than themselves.

—Philippians 2:3, KJV

I didn't hear from my original attorney once my privileges were
reinstated, and this perplexed me since her last e-mail to me
stated, "Mutiny then?" I reached out to her asking about ERO,
CDO, and other legal options to pursue. Eventually, she stated she
didn't think I had a case. Wow! Was she listening to me at all? I
thanked her for her assistance and informed her I planned to move
on to another attorney. She was gracious and professionally acknowledged parting ways.

I interviewed another attorney I learned about who spe-
cialized in large health-care systems ERO cases for a $250.00 fee.
Unfortunately, he missed two of our meetings and was late for the
third, so I decided not to retain him.

I remembered the law partnership, Another Law Firm. I
arranged a consultation for a mere $600.00. Easy come, easy go.
The Lord has provideth. I went for it. I sent documentation to my
new law group for them to review prior to our telephone meeting.
Jackpot! Two attorneys were on the call. They totally understood
my situation, and the big cheese himself wanted to talk with me.

They presented their interpretation of my situation, and I celebrated with enthusiastic exclamations such as, "Wow! You are right on the money!" "You get *it*!" "I never thought anyone could follow me on this big twisted mess!" With delight, they accepted my case. I paid the $6,000.00 retainer with relief. I believed they were the right firm to represent me. God is so good! All the time!

Patience and perseverance paid off. God continually tests me on the subject of patience. Waiting on the Lord has become an expectation, and I simply wait and wait. He is faithful in the end. I learned to lean on Him a long time ago. His blessings are worth leaning on Him, trusting Him, and waiting on Him.

The new attorney's background consisted of political and legal experience. His experience in politics and legal training proved to be the perfect complement in fighting for opioid safety. Best of all, I trusted him.

> "Wait on the LORD: be of good courage, and he shall strengthen thine heart: wait, I say, on the LORD"
>
> —Psalm 27:14, KJV

CHAPTER 13

Grievance Division Office

The LORD is good, a strong hold in the day of trouble;
and he knoweth them that trust in him.

—Nahum 1:7, KJV

I sent the same letter to another office and sought whistle-blower protection. I worked with my new attorney, from the Another Law Office, on this time line and subsequent document.

What Information Was Disclosed
(Describe Whistleblower Disclosure)

1. Dr. Sky disclosed on multiple occasions to chief of staff and center director that medical center patients were taking prescription opioids inappropriately or were diverting opioids that had been prescribed to them. In many cases she disclosed that those patients were allowed to continue taking opioids in violation of state law, sound medical practice, and patient safety.

In the cases of patients diverting their prescriptions, she disclosed that these patients were almost certainly selling those prescription opioids and contributing to the ongoing local opioid epidemic.

Note that discussing any individual patient disclosure necessarily involves examining that patient's confidential medical records. Also note that the dates included at right are not exhaustive, Dr. Sky disclosed similar instances many times since 2015.

2. Fall to Winter 2015

Dr. Sky disclosed to chief of staff that practitioners at the facility were not properly trained in interpreting urine drug screens, and were therefore missing many instances when urine screens were improperly negative. Missing those screens meant that many patients diverting opioids were going undetected (when a drug screen is negative in an opioid patient it means they are not taking the opioids and are likely selling or them or otherwise using them inappropriately).

3. Spring 2016

Dr. Sky disclosed to chief of staff that the medical center was undermining opioid safety efforts by allowing patient advocates to improperly influence medical decisions.

4. Spring 2016

Dr. Sky disclosed to chief of staff that patient advocates are inappropriately pressuring physicians to change opioid safety plans and the volume of opioids dispensed to patients, creating pressure on physicians to prescribe opioids inappropriately and endanger both the safety of those patients and the surrounding community. She disclosed that the medical center administration's support of the patient advocates in disputes about patient opioid prescriptions was leading to inappropriate and unsafe prescriptions against doctors' independent medical judgement.

5. Early Summer 2016

Dr. Sky disclosed to chief of staff that patients were diverting opioids prescribed by the medical center and selling those diverted opioids on medical center grounds.

6. Early Summer 2016

Dr. Sky disclosed to chief of staff that it is unethical and unlawful for the chief of staff or other official to force a physician to write an opioid prescription if the chief of staff approved the reinstatement of opioids and the primary care physician is not in agreement. She stated that such coercion is particularly problematic when the primary care physician believes such a prescription is unethical, unlawful, or unsafe for the patient.

7. Fall 2016

Dr. Sky disclosed to chief of staff that his decision to relocate a patient from one clinic to another clinic over the objections of the original clinic's medical staff, undermined the moral of the original clinic staff and created danger for the particular patient for whom he allowed the transfer. The original clinic medical staff had worked to taper that patient off of opioids and strongly believed that patient only sought a transfer to a new doctor at another clinic in order to keep the patient's current level of opioid prescriptions in place.

8. Very Early Spring 2017

Dr. Sky disclosed to chief of staff that the medical center administration's increasingly frequent practice of overriding primary care physicians' decisions to taper or suspend opioid prescriptions was endangering the health of patients and obstructing their ability to treat patients effectively and that it is a breach of legal and ethical obligations to pressure physicians to provide marinol when their initial decision was against providing this controversial drug.

9. Very Early Spring 2017

Dr. Sky disclosed to chief of staff that the director was harassing and coercing doctors to provide prescriptions to patients after those patients complain about those doctors' medical decision not to provide opioids (or to reduce opioid levels), and that this action was a breach of law, patient safety, and medical ethics.

When Did the Personnel Action Occur?

* Late winter 2016 (leadership day); early spring 2017 (staff meeting); director subjected Dr. Sky to public ridicule in a number of staff meetings and public events.
* Late spring 2017 agency released Dr. Sky's photograph and personal information to a television news reporter and held Dr. Sky up as a scapegoat for large health-care system policies. Director allowed the release of Dr. Sky's photograph without her permission and Dr. Sky did not participate or wish to participate in the story.
* Late spring 2017 agency chief of staff attacked Dr. Sky on the television news story without a basis in fact and held Dr. Sky up as a scapegoat for large health-care system policies.
* Late spring 2017 The agency consented to the television news reporter contacting Dr. Sky, adding a new press relations role to her position that was not part of her duties.
* Late spring 2017: The agency issued a suspension of privileges against Dr. Sky without following the procedure for doing so outlined in policies or facility medical staff bylaws.
* Late spring 2017, Dr. Sky was removed from her position as opioid safety initiative facility co-champion.
* Early summer 2017, another candidate is hired for medical director at East Coast Hospital.
* Early summer 2017 refusal of director to sign for reinstatement of Dr. Sky's privileges following a unanimous recommendation for reinstatement by the Professional Standards Board and Clinical Executive Board on early summer 2017. Director only reinstated Dr. Sky's privileges eleven days later.
* Summer 2017 The chief of staff at the direction of director issues a proposed reprimand against Dr. Sky for failure to follow a medical center policy even though the issues forming the basis of the proposed reprimand were discussed by the Professional Standards Board and Clinical Executive

Board on summer 2017 found to be meritless and chief of staff had approved.

Explain why you believe that the personnel action(s) listed above occurred because of the disclosure(s) that you described. (Be as specific as possible about any dates, locations, names, and positions of all persons mentioned in your explanation. In particular, identify actual and potential witnesses, giving work locations and telephone numbers, if known. Attach a copy of any documents that support your statements. Please provide, if possible, a copy of the notification of the agency s proposal and/ or decision about the personnel action(s) coerced by your complaint. If more space is needed, continue on page.)

The medical center director and chief of staff retaliated against Dr. Sky because her repeated disclosures of instances in which the medical center endangered patients and the community at large by over-prescribing opioids impeded their efforts to pursue high patient satisfaction scores regardless of the cost to patient health.

Despite the growing realization that over-prescription of opioids has become a nationwide epidemic, efforts to solve the problem can still generate vocal opponents. Specifically, patients whose opioid prescriptions are being tapered (e.g. gradually reduced) or suspended (e.g. cut off completely) are frequently unhappy; in many cases because they are addicted. More perniciously, a few patients actively divert opioids (e.g. sell medication rather than take it themselves) and react extremely negatively when their supply is cut off.

Since arriving at the Facility by the River in the fall of 2015, Dr. B. Sky has repeatedly disclosed instances where the medical center's actions were contributing to the opioid crisis. Most of these disclosures were made to chief of staff but many others were made to director as well.

Between Dr. Sky's arrival and the spring of 2017, medical center physicians began prescribing fewer opioids, which created a backlash among patients whose prescriptions were being tapered or suspended. Patient dissatisfaction with physicians' decisions to taper or suspend their opioid prescriptions created a constant stream of complaints to the patient advocates and drove down measures of patient satisfaction.

The medical center's top officials, director and chief of staff were highly sensitive to public criticism of the facility. In particular, the medical center director's job evaluations are directly tied to evaluations of patient satisfaction and he frequently emphasizes the importance of patient satisfaction when communicating with medical center staff.

The backlash against tighter opioid controls manifested in part as a concerted campaign by a few patients against the medical center's opioid reductions, including heavy use of the medical center's patient advocate system, calls to medical center officials, lobbying politicians to intervene, and contacting the news media. These patient protesters' central charge was that doctors were not always meeting with patients before tapering or suspending their opioid prescriptions and they seized on a misinterpretation of a state medical board standard to argue that this practice was inappropriate.

Those protest efforts eventually succeeded in convincing their local politicians to direct the large health-care system to investigate their complaints. Politicians' direction to internal investigators adopted the protesters' self-servingly inaccurate view of state medical board regulations and that inaccurate view ultimately formed the basis of many of the investigation's conclusions. Meanwhile, the protesters succeeded in getting the attention of the local news media as well.

After Dr. Sky's disclosures and conversations to him about opioids, the director frequently stated that he "supports the patients" meaning that when patient satisfaction and opioid safety collided, he gave patients the benefit of the doubt despite the serious safety and legal concerns raised by Dr. Sky. Witnesses: Mr. AO1 and Mr. AO2, administrative officers for primary care. It also shows his clear disagreement with her disclosures and suggests an ad hominem approach to the issue (e.g., his statements strongly implied he believed Dr. Sky does *not* support patients when she raised medical concerns about treatment).

The retaliation against Dr. Sky listed above follows closely in time after a late spring 2017 television local news story discussing the dissatisfied patients' complaints. Days after the local news story aired, the medical center director issued an emergency suspension of privileges in the late spring of 2017. That close connection in time shows the two events were intimately connected. Moreover, that suspension of privileges did not follow either the large health-care system policy or facility medical medical staff bylaws, which also shows that the suspension was retaliatory in nature rather than a proper disciplinary practice.

Further, the medical center's Professional Standards Board and Clinical Executive Board undertook an investigation of the charges against Dr. Sky that supposedly required an emergency suspension. They found the underlying charges to be meritless, recommending Dr. Sky's reinstatement. The director however, initially refused to implement the decision of those boards despite his not being a medical practitioner and not having any clinical expertise, clearly showing a retaliatory motive against Dr. Sky rather than a concern for patient safety or medical center policy. He only relented and signed the reinstatement of her privileges eleven days later when he realized he had no lawful grounds for withholding them.

Subsequently, the medical center retaliated against Dr. Sky again by issuing a proposed reprimand for the same issues it had attempted to suspend her privileges for. This second attempt to discipline Dr. Sky is both an act of retaliation in and of itself, and evidence showing a retaliatory motive because the underlying policies at issue had already been discussed in the prior forum. Attempting to discipline Dr. Sky for a medical practice that the facility's own medical standards boards had found to be proper clearly has no basis in legitimate disciplinary motives.

There is no doubt that these actions were tied directly to Dr. Sky's disclosures on improper opioid practices because the discipline proposed against her was for implementing the tougher opioid practices she called for in her disclosures and, as discussed above, followed just days after negative publicity about tougher opioid practices championed by Dr. Sky. In addition, the agency's decision to discuss Dr. Sky personally in the television news story, even going so far as to distribute her picture without her permission, shows the medical center's clear intent deflect blame on Dr. Sky personally.

In addition, the underlying charges in both the suspension of privileges and proposed reprimand themselves show an improper retaliatory motive for the reasons set forth below:

> First, the medical center has routinely allowed changes to be made to patient opioid prescriptions in supposed violation of the medical board rule as they now interpret it. In particular, between the time when the rule was first issued in 2013 and Dr. Sky's hiring in the fall of 2015, the medical center routinely allowed patient opioid prescriptions to be changed without the meetings they now say the rule requires. Between 2013 and the fall of 2015, Dr. Prior Chief of Staff and Dr. Chief of Staff himself oversaw these routine practices but neither he nor any other employees were disciplined. The Medical Center never cared about these practices until they became a convenient way to retaliate against Dr. Sky, clearly showing retaliation.

> Second, the Medical Center has previously interpreted the medical board opioid rule differently than it did in its discipline against Dr. Sky. In communications to physicians, Dr. CoS explicitly stated that it was ok to make changes to opioid prescriptions even if the supposedly required meetings had not occurred. That sudden change in interpretation clearly shows retaliatory motive because the change was made without examination or explanation. And even, for the sake of argument, if the change in interpretation was an honest one then such an honest change of policy would mean that Dr. Sky should not

have been punished—she was just following the then-current policy.

Third, the Medical Center's interpretation of the state medical board's opioid rule is clearly an incorrect reading of the rule because *under the interpretation put forward by the medical center in its actions against Dr. Sky, any patient who has been prescribed opioids could secure permanent renewals of those prescriptions simply by avoiding a meeting with their physician*. As discussed in depth in the response to proposed removal, such an interpretation is laughable on its face and using that absurd position as the basis for discipline shows the agency's intent was to punish Dr. Sky.

Fourth, when physicians have attempted to meet with every patient in person before tapering or suspending opioid prescriptions, those physicians have found it impossible. In at least one case the medical center has pursued discipline against a physician for inefficiency precisely because she attempted to meet with every patient in person before suspending or tapering opioids. (Witness–Mr. HR Chief) The medical center's lack of regard for its own supposed policy shows that the actions it took against Dr. Sky were clearly retaliatory because if it took those policies seriously, it would support their implementation.

Fifth, it is important to note that Dr. Sky did as much as practically possible to ensure patients were consulted before a change to their opioid prescriptions was made. Specifically, all patients were contacted by the medical center and offered in person appointments to discuss a potential taper or suspension in their opioid prescriptions. The patients who did not have those meetings could have done so had they chose to.

In sum, reducing opioid over-prescription was and is both necessary for patient and community safety, but unpopular with the patients taking those opioids. Dr. Sky's numerous opioid related disclosures made her a target for medical center leadership, particularly when they were placed under pressure by unhappy patients, and she was targeted for retaliation as a result.

What action would you like GDO to take in this matter (that is, what remedy are you asking for)?

Compensatory damages for: change in salary, mental distress, worsening of medical conditions, irreparable damage to reputation; attorneys' fees

By winter of 2017, the Grievance Division Office turned over the case to my attorney. Our next step begins the next journey toward revealing the truth regarding actions by politicians and large health-care system executives. The Legal Battle Board would be our next step toward exposing the wrongs regarding the actions by official leaders and their role in perpetuating the opioid epidemic in America. Won't anybody listen?

> "No weapon that is formed against thee shall prosper; and every tongue that shall rise against thee in judgement thou shalt condemn. This is the heritage of the servants of the LORD, and their righteousness is of me, saith the LORD"
> —Isaiah 54:17, KJV

CHAPTER 14

The Return of the Ignorant Oversight Body

When a man's ways please the LORD, he maketh
even his enemies to be at peace with him.

—Proverbs 16:7, KJV

The Ignorant Oversight Body (IOB) returned to our facility in the fall of 2017. This time they were investigating the chief of staff. Many of the leaders from the facility were interviewed that day. The following is my account as it follows transcripts:

Dr. Sky: I have a lot to say. I don't know where you want to start.

Investigator: We can start with the perception of the concerns about a hostile work environment.

Dr. Sky: There is no doubt that there is a hostile work environment. I reported this over a 90-minute appointment in the early spring of 2017 to the chief of staff. The director's unprofessional behavior is very embarrassing during leadership meetings to many of us. Especially to me. He has been very embarrassing to the administrative officer for the deputy chief of staff publicly and during our service line weekly meetings. The director and also the chief of staff are always there too...when I bring up opioid safety concerns and when we do our weekly service line reports, we often include opioid safety information.

Opioid safety initiative implementation falls under primary care. He (the director) will say, "I always believe the patients" (when they complain to him about opioid medication changes). Despite the fact that over…I can tell you some numbers…over five-month period of time, when I first got here I found diversion and doctor shopping going on and other disturbing related patient unsafe behavior. And it was seven-two patients within the first five months, that I discovered diversion, overdosing, multiple opioid prescribers, patients chewing fentanyl patches, patients snorting opioid medication, patients hospitalized for respiratory depression, and patients that died from unintentional overdoses. Beyond that timeframe, I don't have any data. When I was checking on things

Investigator: Let me interrupt. Are the seven-two patients the and patient's that you were providing direct care for?

Dr. Sky: And this is where we might have to agree to disagree. Your report, which I have with me, is in my opinion and I do want to go on record as saying, very flawed. Your report says that I did not include nursing staff in my notes…that nurses stumbled upon my notes. That is not true at all.

All of us primary care providers, if anything, we overuse nursing because we have a provider shortage. I felt badly because the nurses were caught in the middle of upset patients. I have all the documentation that can show that nurses were very informed and actively participated in discussions with patients. The patients were not "cut off at the knees" which has been publicly proclaimed in the media. The chief of staff participated on a television news report in the late spring of 2017. This facility had to go through the director and release my photo, violating privacy laws and policy. The director released my picture without my permission, and the newscaster repeatedly stated that I "cut people off (of opioids) at the knees" as my photograph repeatedly appeared. The patients on the interview were not truthful and that is all I can say about that due to HIPAA. All of the patients received medical assistance and this is very well documented. This fact has been proven based upon two professional clinical reviews of all of the clinic charts I touched by two clinical professional oversight committees. The care I provided proved to be very appropriate care with some of the reviewers stating I "deserved a medal for my opioid safety initiative dedication".

Investigator: Going back to the hostile work environment
Dr. Sky: And that's what I am getting to. So that was a very hostile interview (the television news report). The chief of staff chimed right in there...failing to disclose all of our efforts to apply opioid safety...knowing full well that I was a champion of addressing this very important epidemic. This whole facility (except for the executive leadership team), all of the providers, which are many...the community, the media in general, newspapers in general understand the need to address the opioid epidemic... Many providers were very upset by the lack of support from senior leaders because there was clinical justification for their actions and serious consequences for not applying safety measures.

Every single patient—because I reviewed all the charts that were reviewed, either had an appointment or was offered a face-to-face visit the next day or at least within a couple of weeks. Nurses were always informed to help relay the messages. Anyway, nobody checked their facts. And I am going to go on record to say that the politician had her hands all over this catastrophe. She created fear and misused her power using coercion to influence the medical center director to accomplish what she wanted to accomplish. The director complied due to ambitions of his own.

The director in turn used fearful tactics and power of coercion to order the chief of staff to apply unethical and unprofessional punishment onto people such as me. I am probably the number one "scapegoat" in all this. You ask any of the other service line leaders and chiefs... I think that I am the facility "scapegoat" should come out in this investigation. Most people know that I advocated for opioid safety and supported primary care providers and other clinical staff in doing the right things in regards to dispensing opioids for chronic pain.

Investigator: Dr. Sky, regarding a hostile work environment, your photograph was provided without your consent to the public?
Dr. Sky: Yes.

Again, I met with the chief of staff. I asked to meet with him. I was basically doing an exit interview. He knew that I could no longer put up with a hostile work environment.

The director influences the chief of staff who I think is probably fearful for his job. So, it is not just the chief of staff involved. The director is at the steering wheel and the chief of staff is put in the middle. However, if I were the chief of staff, I would not compromise my medical integrity or my professional integrity and this is where we differ. As far as how the political reviews work, our office handles every single one of the inquiries that relates to primary care. That is why I know what is going on. Any complaint that comes through the chief of staff's office or any kind of complaint that comes to politician's or the director's office, we review it.

Investigator: With regards to the Professional Standards Board, can you talk to us about what you know about that?
Dr. Sky: I am actually the person that is probably being referenced. I know that the Ignorant Oversight Body—I am sorry but your report is a very inaccurate report, I just have to say that for the record and to help educate all of you. The initial IOB report is very inaccurate. But it is probably based on what you were told. I can prove that the report is inaccurate.

The IOB report was released in the early spring of 2017 I have since learned. Then a few days later the news report was released and my privileges were suspended. And there are issues with that it still

143

gets to me (voice breaks). I was away at the time, because I studied for and completed a board recertification examination in family medicine.

I was also buying a house at this time. I had a new job at another facility, a promotion. As for your question about 90 minutes, this refers to the very early spring of 2017 meeting with the chief of staff when I gave my exit interview to the chief of staff and said that I can't work a hostile work environment. I informed him I was most likely going to file an ERO complaint which I've since done. I filed because of the hostile work environment.

Plus, I see what they (the executive leadership team) do to other people and their actions are unprofessional and unethical. So those events, the IOB report and television news story, came out in close proximity. Then, there was all this hubbub. Unaware of any of this chaos at this time, I spent time researching the time table of events. Then there was—like the very next day, the hot news article summaries that went to headquarters of the large health-care facility for review. Then the chief pain person from headquarters, I can't remember his name, he wanted to get information from our facility. I was away so I was not included to help set the record straight. This was still in the spring of 2017. I was then interviewed by the Accountability Office to the Ignorant Oversight Body and the interviewers included a clerical person and a physician. This occurred the day I got back to the facility in the spring. The very next day I received the summary suspension notice. I was cited for not practicing opioid safety.

Until I arrived at this facility, nobody practiced opioid safety to any considerable degree. The summary suspension issuance seemed so ridiculous. The Professional Standards Board was not included in the review of the proposal. I know that our medical staff bylaws and policy regarding credentialing and privileging outline the process for issuing a summary suspension. The director and the chief of staff did not follow large health-care system processes and procedures. The director ordered the chief of staff to give me to a summary suspension. The chief of staff said that he agreed to do it. I was flabbergasted. The chief of staff teared up when he gave it to me. He had a tear in his eye. I had a tear in my eye. He knew it was wrong.

Investigator: What happened after that?

Dr. Sky: So, after that, I retained an attorney. Just on policy and bylaws alone, the suspension was wrong. Plus, anyone in leadership...

Interviewer: Were there questions specifically about your decisions, your clinical decisions?

Dr. Sky: Everybody, as in only the executive leadership team, thought I should meet with the patients face-to-face. You can't. It's like the chief of staff, the deputy chief of staff, and the person acting in the position since I had been out on sick leave now realize that you don't meet with all the patients when you decide to do a renewal or a change of medication when you are covering many different locations.

As opioid safety champion, I couldn't be at all of those places to do face-to-face visits for every request. And that's the big beef... doctors and nursing staff, should understand clinically, if there is no drug in the urine, you are just wasting an appointment to see them face-to-face to tell them that there is no drug in your urine. You wouldn't do that (waste an appointment). This is not standard of care when access at the large health-care system is such a big issue... Also, you would not meet with the patient face-to-face to tell him that you discovered that he/she was getting medication at sixteen different locations in the community. There is no needed evaluation or assessment for that discovery. I acknowledge that someone does need to tell the patient about the finding; however, the provider often relies on social workers, nursing staff, clinical pharmacy specialist, and other members of the team to communicate to the patient.

And if there needs to be any tapers and this is the other concern, everyone is generalizing the term, "tapering," to mean these three things: finding no drug in the urine, getting opioids from multiple providers in the community, and reducing medication doses. These are three different scenarios. However, the IOB report lumped them altogether, completely misleading the readers of the report. Worse yet, people with power acted on this inaccurate report which resulted in a knowledgeable, supportive, caring employee becoming a "scape-goat" for the facility.

Now as for tapering, I had a guy with a prolonged QTC (heart issue) on his EKG that was not previously addressed. We cannot give him the full medication dose because of the finding because he could develop a heart arrhythmia and die. I first had to do an EKG and when I got the EKG back out was like oh my goodness. We had to taper him down as in decrease his methadone dose to prevent death. I said please tell the patient to the nurse and I will consult the clinical pharmacy specialist who will be in touch with him. Many clinical people communicated for me. I couldn't physically do it all and the patient knew the medical home team nurse. The clinical pharmacy specialist, here is his name in case you ever want to speak with him and he would be a great one to talk to by the way... He would contact patient right away and explain why the tapering (as in reducing the methadone dose) was occurring and what to expect at that time. I also offered face-to-face visits with a covering provider. The majority of the patients did come in for face-to-face visits. I was criticized on the IOB report for not being the one to do see the patient right away when I was making the change. I couldn't and as the opioid safety consultant, I would not be expected to see everyone face-to-face at many different locations. We were down many providers and one person just can't be in all those places at once. I provided coverage by other providers and this is all that should have been expected. Why the IOB team thought I needed to be present is beyond my comprehension. I believe you all were misled by disgruntled nurses from the clinic. The Administrative Board interviewed me at the same time you all did and came to the completely opposite conclusion. They reported that the nursing staff was disgruntled and were put in an uncomfortable position and my clinical judgement was not questioned. The internal and external clinical reviews of all of the clinic charts supported my clinical judgement and was not questioned.

Understand that I would get people to cover for absent providers. I would plug the holes in. I had two covering fee-based as providers who would assist along with other providers.

I'm going to tell you as the opioid safety champion, I earned the trust and respect of the pharmacists, my primary care staff, mental health providers, social workers, and suicide prevention coordinators. Here are the names and you can contact them for verification. A provider would call me regarding a patient we were trying to taper and then the patient would go and somehow get the ear of the chief of staff. The chief of staff approached providers to try to get them to increase the opioid dose, stop the taper (decreasing of the dose), or restart opioids which were all suggestions which would result in inappropriate clinical actions. I saw one really good example where the chief of staff seriously asked a provider to rewrite an opioid for somebody who we knew was addicted. We were doing this really prolonged taper and she had a known addiction problem.

And of course, we offer all the help in the world. We want to help people. We really do. The primary care provider documented in the medical record, "I do not agree with restarting medications." The chief of staff asked the provider to increase the opioid dose and stop the taper. The primary care provider said, "I do not agree." The chief of staff did not release opioid medications under his own name. The prescription was released under the primary care provider's name. The chief of staff doesn't even have a DEA license. I think the action by the chief of staff is illegal.

Investigator: Anything else?

Dr. Sky: You brought up complaints about employees leaving the large health-care system...you talk about people leaving the facility for this injustice. I mean I'm definitely going. My privileges were reinstated at the facility and now I feel forced to leave the large health-care system, less than one year short of a full retirement. This political stuff is crazy. Politics can ruin your career. I can't get a job with—I mean you "google" my name and all this stuff comes up. It is so unfair. I do nothing but protect the community and patients. I am all about medicine and doing safe medicine. If anybody doesn't get it from all the publicity regarding our country's opioid safety epidemic...believe me, I honestly don't think the director gets it at all. Or the chief of staff. The politician who has done a 180 degree turn on her approach to all this...She doesn't even check her facts. She just reacts. She is using me and the large health-care system as a political platform to get reelected. Disgusting. This is a national epidemic. I hope my story someday gets told.

The remaining documentation went on to clarify information presented. It was clear to me by this time that I was dealing with incompetent people. I previously sent the Accountability Office to the Ignorant Oversight Body more than enough documentation proving the accuracy of my testimony. One of the investigators continues to misunderstand the situation. The two physicians on the panel were argumentative and accusatory in nature. Who can trust our oversight committees when they are composed of ineffectual panel members?

> "And he answered, Fear not: for they that be with
> us are more than they that be with them"
> —2 Kings 6:16, KJV

CHAPTER 15

Subcommittee on Oversight
and Investigation

Let us hold fast the profession of our faith without
wavering; (for he is faithful that promised).

—Hebrews 10:23, KJV

In the fall of 2017, my attorney and I met Ms. RN, health subcommittee leader, and Mr. Attorney, subcommittee staff director and counsel, by telephone. The goal of the call was to have the chance for me to talk with Ms. RN about my concerns that there is danger to the community regarding opioid-prescribing practices at our facility. The interpretation of state medical law is wrong and dangerous. We needed to rectify the interpretation for the safety of the community. I had the chance to share confidential information without repercussion. My attorney would have the opportunity to speak with Mr. Attorney about the legal aspects of misinterpreting state medical law. If physicians did not act on inappropriately negative urine drug screens and continued to prescribe opioids, they would have lost their medical licenses. If physicians continued to prescribe to patients who were visiting eighteen different medical practices, receiving opioids at each practice, they would have lost their licenses. If physicians continued to prescribe opioids to known addicts, they would have lost their licenses. Requiring face-to-face visits in these instances is a waste of resources and not the standard of care.

I discussed the flawed IOB report with Ms. RN. I reviewed my visit with the Accountability Office to the Ignorant Oversight Body team as a result of the flawed Ignorant Oversight Body report. I recapped all the documentation I sent to the non-clinician as part of the AO-IOB interview. I reviewed the shortcomings of the IOB report, especially the chart that was used and prepared by the clerical staff.

I explained that the Administrative Board (AB) interview for the clinic took place at the same time as the Ignorant Oversight Body (IOB) review and that they came to completely different conclusions. The AB group determined that the nurses felt harassed by patients. I agreed and stated that I apologized to the nurses on two occasions in person because I knew this was hard on them. When some patients choose to sell their prescriptions and this is discovered, doctors can no longer be their supplier. In fact, these patients should be reported to the police to be investigated; but the facility chose not to do this at the time even though it was in the policy. These patients become desperate, angry, and sometimes explosive when they lose their income in particular. For some reason, some feel entitled to the medication to do as they please I have heard repeatedly. I feel for them not having a source of income; but they chose an inappropriate way to make money that is illegal. I expected them to feel embarrassed when they were caught diverting; but this was not the emotion I generally witnessed.

Nursing statements in the IOB report were false statements. One nurse stated that I did not ever inform the nursing staff of the recommended changes and they "stumbled" onto my notes. The opposite is true. I informed the nursing staff every time through co-signature requirement, and this is easy to prove; just read the charts. The clinical reviews on the charts proved that I informed the nurses every time. The nursing staff was unforgiving and vengeful. They did not appreciate the patients' behaviors and blamed me for taking action. They obviously did not want to have the hard conversations with patients although in other regards, they wanted to be part of the team. In reality, the nurses should have been resentful toward the provider I was covering for due to his inappropriate prescribing habits (which I addressed as his supervisor). I forgave the nursing staff because they were not educated about opioid safety prior to my arrival. I still do not believe nursing leadership engages in opioid safety initiatives which is alarming.

Lastly, I reported Dr. CoS's false testimony under oath to the Accountability Office to the Ignorant Oversight Body (AO-IOB). Again, can you say perjury?

Ms. RN shared that she previously met me on a site visit to our facility in the past. I instantly remembered and stated, "I remember! You were very supportive of my opioid safety initiative implementation results."

I sent the oversight committee medical staff information through my attorney that Ms. RN and Mr. Attorney requested including names of providers to interview and examples of what my attorney and I call "holy cow" messages regarding coercion by the director and chief of staff to prescribe opioids inappropriately.

The oversight committee medical staff RN agreed to be a support for the primary care providers in my absence. I informed her of my report of concern to the internal inspectors because the facility no longer had an opioid safety-prescribing champion to oversee opioid safety in my absence. The acting ACOS for primary care who was officially the deputy chief of staff was appointed this duty; but he is acting on behalf of the director and the chief of staff expecting providers to prescribe opioids inappropriately to appease angry patients.

My attorney reviewed the misinterpretation of state medical law as well as the actual and potential consequences. He requested assistance during the second IOB investigation and clarification of state medical and other laws to the IOB team. The second IOB investigation is presently ongoing as of early winter of 2017.

We sent patient examples to the oversight committee medial staff and legal members for their review as requested. I am only including the summary of the content to comply with Health Insurance Portability and Accountability Act of 1996 (HIPAA).

In late fall of 2017, in the evening, my attorney wrote:

Ms. RN and Mr. Attorney,

To follow up on our conversation a few weeks ago about inappropriate opioid prescription practices at the facility I am about to forward a few emails in response to your request for written documentation of the medical center leadership's encouragement of opioid over-prescription.

Out of respect for your time I have included short descriptions of what each email contains at the beginning of each of the individual emails. Of the five, the first titled "Medical Center CoS Giving Addicted Patient Opioids After Taper Was Complete" is the closest I've seen to a smoking gun and I encourage you to start there.

In addition, I am sending another email with a list of witnesses the subcommittee, the IOB, or whatever alternative investigator you alert can contact for in-depth verbal testimony.

Finally, I am planning on submitting FOIA requests for the complete interview transcripts of all of the IOB, internal inspections, and other investigations into the medical center. While the agency should be legally obligated to share those transcripts, many agencies can be reluctant to answer a FOIA request. If you are authorized to request and share those transcripts with me I would appreciate it very much as it would save quite a bit of trouble.

Feel free to contact Dr. Sky or me if you have any questions about the following emails or the situation at the facility in general and thank you for your interest and concern regarding the issue.

Mr. Attorney
attorney address

--

Mr. Oversight Attorney
Attorney

(1 of 5)

The email chain below shows the medical center chief of staff telling a known addict he can resume a morphine prescription after his morphine taper was already complete. Note the bottom email in the chain describing his erratic behavior including intentionally driving his car into a building.

From Dr. Sky:

This patient was tapered off of morphine due to known addiction. Mental Health and others assisted. He had knee and hip arthritis diagnosis. He had a suicide attempt so this alone would be a reason not to even consider opioids, especially in the face of known addiction. Many alternative treatments have been offered. He cancels appointments and is difficult to contact. We had to send out the police for a welfare check on him.

[copy of email chain below is attached as well]

(2 of 5)

This is an example of a patient who likely died because of inappropriate opioid prescription by the large health-care system.

He was admitted to a private hospital for aspiration pneumonia suspected to be the result of the use of opioids he received from the large health-care system. He died during that hospital admittance. The private medical practitioner treating him was so concerned about the patient's opioid prescriptions that they called the large health-care system to flag it as inappropriate and recommend it be stopped.

Dr. Sky immediately alerted medical center leadership at the time to the situation and told them it was an example of her concerns about opioid over-prescription.

[see attached]

(3 of 5)

From Dr. Sky:

These attachments reference ongoing attempts by Dr. CoS to slow xxs taper and reinstate opioids. As a medical team, we have met to discuss best treatment for this patient. She is clearly addicted to opioids and will not accept treatment. Mr. Director is very involved too and not a clinician. Dr. Chief of Staff (CoS) follows direction from Mr. Director and this is extremely concerning.

[NOTE 1: Page 1 of attached document "xx Prescription Record" states that Dr. PCP filled the prescription at the direction of the Medical Center CoS and not his own medical judgement.]
[NOTE 2: The doctor involved in this case, Dr. PCP has been included on the list of potential people to interview and can provide more details about the case.]
The email below was sent by Dr. PCP to Dr. Sky telling her that he was forced by CoS to stop weaning the patient off of opioids against his medical judgement.
Attachments further document the interaction with CoS.

-----Original Message-----

From: Dr. PCP
To: Dr. B. Sky
Sent: Tue, early summer of 2017 in the am
Subject: letter B.

I am still working on a draft of the letter. I have a phone call with xx tomorrow, and won't send the letter until we talk. As for the patient xx I was forced to stop the weaning and resume a higher dosing schedule; I have asked to be recused- very complicated problem! You may want to do a little research at xxxx; in 2016 Ms. Politician did an interview and absolutely threw our clinic under the narc bus; my response to that was what got me in trouble, and likely is a major factor in today's situation. As for your book, how about this for a title: "Oh, the things they like to hide!"

More to follow…
Reply All Forward

(4 of 5)

The email below is an example of the medical center leadership's policy of improperly prescribing opioids, in this case, by allowing a transfer away from a primary care physician who did not want to prescribe opioids to the patient.

Note that this particular patient was first switched away from Dr. PCP1 after she would not prescribe him opioids, then later asked to be transferred back to her.

Dr. PCP1 is included on the list of potential witnesses.

From: Sky, B.
Sent: Spring 2017 AM
To: DCOS
Subject: RE: PCP re-Assignment.

Dr. DCOS,

I know Dr. PCP1 and she will not restart opiates for chronic pain. I will not force the PC providers to write for medications they do not agree to write. Dr. PCP1 and Dr. PCP2 are strong providers. You may have made the patient happy by giving opiates for the short term; but this will most likely not be continued and the patient will most likely complain again to get more opiates…cycle of complaints will most likely continue in my opinion based upon a wealth of experience.

Thanks for trying to help. We probably need to talk and perhaps include primary care providers. I welcome you to come to our PC provider meetings.

B.

Dr. B. Sky

Associate chief of staff, Primary Care

From: DCOS
Sent: Spring 2017 PM
To: Sky, B.
Subject: PCP re-Assignment.

B.

Can you please consider Mr.xxx#xxxx to reassign/switch back to Dr. PCP1 as per his preference and wishes after long angry discussion today as you might know pt has been very unhappy for some time. Thanks.

Dr. DCOS

Deputy Chief of Staff

(5 of 5) is not included for privacy reasons

CHAPTER 16

Patient Record Safety Flags

And therefore will the LORD wait, that he may be
gracious unto you, and therefore will he be exalted, that
he may have mercy upon you: for the LORD is a God
of judgement: blessed are they that wait for him.

—Isaiah 30:18, KJV

I placed seventy-two patient record flags on charts since my arrival to the facility by the river from the fall of 2015 to the spring of 2016. The facility has placed over 350 patient opioid safety record flags through the fall of 2017 and is now reviewing each and every flag. The director wants all of the opioid safety flags removed; but engaged clinicians are fighting this order.

I put opioid safety flags on thirty-seven charts for inappropriately negative urine drug screens, there was no drug when there should have been drug, when the patients were filling their opioids monthly on time. Twenty-five patients were found to be "double dipping," filling opioids at multiple locations and the facility simultaneously, which was uncovered by checking the state Prescription Monitoring Program database which had not been a common practice prior to my arrival and under the leadership of the chief of staff. One patient filled 1,200 opioid pills in one month. Another patient went to thirteen different medical offices and received opioids, and another saw fifteen different community providers seeking opioid prescriptions; another patient visited six different community providers at six different medical practices; still another patient saw seven different providers in four different cities using three pharmacies in the state to fill opioid prescriptions. Four patients were significantly short on opioid pill or patch counts; four patients had active addiction problems; six were cannabinoid or other illicit drug users; four patients previously overdosed on their opioid medications and were still receiving opioid prescriptions regularly; one patient had a previous suicide attempt using opioid medication as the vehicle and continued to receive opioids for chronic pain; one patient was inappropriately positive for amphetamines (he was not prescribed amphetamines, but he was ingesting amphetamines or meth); one snorted his pills. Two patients used oxygen, and they were taking significant doses of opioids to create respiratory depression and death. One of the two patients died from respiratory depression while on opioids for chronic pain. Mental health providers and suicide prevention coordinators were actively assisting thirty-six of the patients. One patient died using multiple fentanyl patches. Two other patients were arrested for selling their opioid prescriptions in the community and went to jail. Five patients sought help for addiction from the facility following the placement of the opioid safety flags.

The chief of staff was aware of these findings. The director did not want to pay attention to these discoveries. I tried to disclose my concerns regarding these patients. The director ignored me.

CHAPTER 17

The Legal Battle

And we know that all things work together for good to them that love God, to them who are the called according to his purpose.

—Romans 8:28, KJV

I t is noteworthy to mention that as of the winter of 2017, three primary care providers, the administrative officer for primary care, and the associate chief of staff for primary care left the facility by the river. Four of us left the large health-care system altogether, discouraged and frustrated. Another employee relocated to another facility out of the state. A talented primary care nurse practitioner left primary care to work in specialty medicine. Other primary care providers are seeking opportunities outside of primary care and the facility by the river. They keep in contact with me, and I happily give them glowing references. The stamina of the primary care providers at this facility and other locations across the country impresses me.

I am now working in the private sector as a primary care provider. I wonder why I waited so long. The difference in navigating the private medical world astonishes me. There are now many outpatient positions without "on call." Despite all of the publicity that follows me, I had employment opportunities in the end. Initially, I felt beaten up, hopeless, and shameful until I realized I did not create this state of affairs. I participated in opioid safety as part of the solution. I applied my experience, shared lessons learned and best practices, and supported primary care and others of the medical staff.

The Lord truly blessed us with a relocation to the big sky country out west. We live in a house on a hill, my dream ever since I can remember. Our home looks like a lodge with mountain views from every window. Tall pine trees loom alongside the aspens. A creek filled with trout and other fish bubbles through our property below creating soothing sounds of comfort as we appreciate God's work of nature.

My husband continues to drive me to work every day, and others have fun calling me "princess." I fondly remember another "princess" from my time spent at Facility by the River Health Care System and her encouragement. I smile. I praise God for all of the storms and for bringing David and me to where we now live. We rejoice and remind each other that all of the previous turmoil and suffering will result in God's glory. I love caring for patients on a full-time basis once again. My four-day workweek allows David and me to explore the western frontier. There are real cowboys out here!

My lawsuit against the large health-care system continues, and my hearing date is established. David and I look forward to the day when this legal battle is behind us. I can tell David feels helpless at times and the battle wears on him. I know the battle wears on me. Just as we start to give into our weariness, we remember what a privilege it is to be used by God in this fight to address opioid safety in the name of saving lives. We trust God. God is faithful. Therefore, we press on.

Acronyms

AB   Administrative Board
ACOS   Associate Chief of Staff
AO   Administrative Officer
AO-IOB   Accountability Office to the Ignorant Oversight Body
CDC   Center for Disease Control
CDO   Complaint Department Office
CEB   Clinical Executive Board
COS   Chief of Staff
CPAP   Continuous Positive Airway Pressure
DCOS   Deputy Chief of Staff
ED   Emergency Department
ELT   Executive Leadership Team
ERO   Equal Rights Organization
ES   Employee Survey
FMLA   Family and Medical Leave Act
FOIA   Freedom of Information Act
FPPE   Focused Professional Practice Evaluation
GI Bill   This is a bill passed in 1944 for bringing educational benefits to World War II Veterans and still exists
GDO   Grievance Division Office
HFO   Hassle Free Office
HIPAA   Health Insurance Portability and Accountability Act of 1996
IOB   Ignorant Oversight Body
ICU   Intensive Care Unit
LBB   Legal Battle Board
MBA   Master of Business Administration
OC   Outpatient Clinic

OPPE	Ongoing Professional Practice Evaluation
OSI	Opioid Safety Initiative
PCP	Primary Care Provider
PMP	Prescription Monitoring Program
PSB	Professional Standards Board
RN	Registered Nurse
VTel	Video Telecommunications

ABOUT THE AUTHOR

D r. B. Sky, a professing Christian since her teenage years, joined a medical team in big sky country in the late fall of 2017 following a fifteen-year struggle fighting with political, media, and management powers about the existence of an opioid epidemic at the large health-care system. She tirelessly and successfully worked to establish opioid safety initiatives at several medical facilities. Her fight involved preventing unintentional opioid overdoses to save lives. She relocated to the west on faith with her encouraging husband, David, following years of adversity addressing opioid safety concerns with unrelenting retaliatory large health-care system leaders.

Dr. Sky worked for the large organization and related agencies for almost twenty years. She first served as a general medical officer for the military at a submarine base. Following four years of private practice in a small town on the east coast, Dr. B. Sky accepted a position as a primary care physician for the Great Lakes Medical Center. After receiving her MBA in health care, Dr. Sky relocated to a health-care system in the land of corn and soybeans. She served as the primary and specialty care service line director for five years until she was recruited by the Facility by the River Health Care System as associate chief of staff for primary care and opioid safety facility champion until she retired.

Dr. B. Sky's significant accomplishments included partnering with a Midwest farm to develop the Veteran's Salute! Program for Veterans as part of the therapeutic horseback riding and driving program in the Midwest. She traveled with Veterans to see their memorials in Washington, DC, as part of the Midwest Honor Flight team. She volunteered in the community as the medical director for the pregnancy support center. Lastly, Dr. B. Sky worked as a leader to apply opioid safety initiatives at the large health-care system to help with the opioid epidemic. She continues to work with leaders in Washington, DC, to ensure that physicians are able to apply opioid safety measures, unhindered, in order to protect the community from unintentional overdose.

Welcome to big sky country where God's blessings abound!

CPSIA information can be obtained
at www.ICGtesting.com
Printed in the USA
LVHW090149120719
623885LV00001B/31/P